REBORN THAT WAY

One Woman, One Faith & Countless Miracles

Laurie Campbell

NORTH STAR HARBINGER
Wilmington, Delaware

Copyright © 2013 by Laurie Campbell
All rights reserved.

North Star Harbinger
2711 Centerville Road, Suite 120
PMB 6132
Wilmington, DE 19808
www.northstarlds.org

Publisher's Note: This is a true story. Some names are actual while others are fictitious in order to help retain anonymity.

Reborn That Way/ Laurie Campbell – 1st ed.
ISBN: 978-0615806341

*To my husband
who loves me, not in spite of my past,
but because of it.*

"This mighty change is not simply the result of working harder... Rather, it is the consequence of a fundamental change in our desires, our motives, and our natures made possible through the Atonement of Christ the Lord."

–ELDER DAVID A. BEDNAR

INTRODUCTION

In 1990, I began writing a book titled *Born That Way? A True Story of Overcoming Same-Sex Attraction*. It was based upon the doctrine of The Church of Jesus Christ of Latter-day Saints. Three years later, I submitted the completed manuscript to Deseret Book who published it as their first book on the topic.

The book garnered some press as well as reader comments. Those who were dealing with unwanted same-sex attractions and other desires outside the Lord's boundaries expressed gratitude. Critics resented my implications that sexual orientation, as currently defined, could change. They insisted I was suppressing my true homosexual orientation and attractions. They presumed to know my feelings better than I, insisting that I'd give way to the instinctual drive of my "true nature," like the swallow returning to Capistrano, I suppose.

One critic challenged me to write a sequel to *Born That Way* in 10 more years because I wouldn't be able to maintain my "newly-found orientation" for very long.

Well, it has now been 20 years since I wrote the book and I've continued to maintain my newly-found orientation. I am still oriented toward the Savior's eternal gospel plan. I no longer consider myself to be gay or lesbian, I have not returned to same-sex relationships, nor do I want to.

Toward the completion of the initial manuscript, I met the man who became my husband and eternal companion. We are still in love and deeply committed to each other and the gospel, 20 years later. We are also raising three children born within the new and everlasting covenant.

We've endured some heart-wrenching trials and marital difficulties, none of which are related to my earlier sexual orientation and identity.

Although my emotional and sexual attractions were in transition while I wrote the book, I did not talk about changing from a homosexual to a bisexual or a heterosexual. Those terms are important for some people, but they can be restrictive labels for others, misrepresenting the intricate tapestry and fluidity of human sexuality.

I do not identify as gay or ex-gay, bisexual or heterosexual. I am a daughter of God.

Born That Way described the most significant change we can undergo – the mighty change of heart. I turned away from desires and behaviors outside the Lord's boundaries, including but not limited to same-sex attraction, and began to desire only those things within the Lord's boundaries. I obeyed gospel principles with greater exactness and a commitment to the future rather than looking back and longing for the past. As my righteousness increased, I discovered a more intimate relationship with the Savior as well as a more abundant life.

I've learned I cannot talk about the change from my past lesbian relationships and gay identity to becoming a faithful Latter-day Saint who married in the temple without being accused by some of being a bigot, a liar, and/or anti-gay. I respect the freedom of religion, belief systems, and perspectives of others. That includes those who feel that once gay, always gay, and the only way to true happiness and fulfillment is through gay relationships. However, I have experienced life differently, and I know other people who have, too.

I cannot emphasize enough how my experiences are not necessarily the same as others. I have heard of instances where my first book was used to attack some Mormons who identify as gay and lesbian: "Look. This lady 'changed her sexual orientation.' Why don't you?" Or, "See. Homosexuality really is a choice and you can simply choose not to." Both of those statements are harmful.

I'm not saying that all Latter-day Saints, whatever their previous attractions, will meet someone of the opposite sex to whom they are attracted and wish to marry. The gospel requires that we turn our will and our future over to God, faithfully accepting whatever "the Lord seeth fit to inflict upon"[1] us, along with whatever blessings he might have in store. That may not include a temple marriage in this life. Then again, it might. Either way, trials are inevitable.

"Strong faith in the Savior is submissively accepting of His will and timing in our lives—even if the outcome is not what we hoped for or wanted."[2]

A marriage with someone of the opposite sex should only take place if a person is emotionally, spiritually, romantically, and physically attracted to him or her. And if attractions to the same sex continue or reoccur in the marriage, it's important to remember temptations are a crucial part of The Plan, in whatever form they take.

Unfortunately, some people with homosexual attractions have been advised to marry someone even when the attractions weren't there. The results have been disastrous. Fortunately, several Church leaders have stated that marriage is not to be viewed as some sort of "solution."

I've often been asked whether or not I think people are born that way, born with tendencies that may contribute to various desires and behaviors, including homosexual attractions. My answer is yes, most likely. The definition of repentance in the LDS Bible Dictionary states: "Since we are born into conditions of mortality, repentance comes to mean a turning of the heart and will to God, and a renunciation of sin to which we are naturally inclined."[3]

Desires to sin are a natural part of the human experience. However, that doesn't mean God wants us to act on those desires. Nor are we helpless or compelled to act upon them. They are weaknesses designed to become strengths.

Many of my weaknesses have become strengths through the power of the Atonement and lots of hard work.

Modern scientists have discovered that socialization, aggression, the drive to accomplish or succeed, alcoholism, intelligence, all sorts of things can be affected by genetics. Biological factors help shape human behavior. Fortunately, biology is not destiny.

Human beings are affected by many different factors that often change across the lifespan. Each one of us is a unique combination of thoughts, feelings, behaviors, self-identity, spiritual identity, age, hormones, brain chemistry, personality traits, culture, past and present circumstances, our perceptions of past and present circumstances, as well as a host of other contributing factors.

The old debate pitting nature against nurture is finally being put to rest. It is now obvious that genetics, environment and life experiences work in combination to influence our likes and our dislikes, our passions and repulsions, our desires and aversions, for better and for worse. That's not even taking into account the strongest influence of all for many Latter-day Saints—our spiritual orientation and identity as well as our faith in Jesus Christ and His ability to help transform lives.

The Lord has asked us to put off "the natural man."[4] That includes unrighteous desires as well as the erroneous conclusion that we can't do anything about those desires. It can be difficult to believe or fully understand Jesus Christ when He promises that we can put off the natural man, in this life, and become spiritually reborn.

If we identify with our earthly desires and natural selves rather than our spiritual selves, we limit our potential. We may say: "I am bulimic." "I am an addict." "I am quick-tempered." "I am weak." "I am gay." And all the while, the Great I Am stands before us, and within us, calling us to something beyond our mortal condition. He reminds us that we were with Him long before we were with the world. He calls us to become, not as we will, but as "I AM."

When we consciously or subconsciously adopt other identities, our challenge is to transform them so they are in harmony with our true, spiritual identity. In other words, the body is to conform to the spirit, not vice versa.

Repentance involves putting off the natural man, along

with its natural desires, and gaining a "fresh view of ourselves, God and the world."[5] For Latter-day Saints seeking to overcome desires to sin, a vital first step and strength throughout the process is gained by remembering that our true, enduring identity is that of valiant children of our Heavenly Parents. It's important to gain a fresh view of ourselves as spiritual beings, first and foremost, striving to overcome sinful tendencies.

The process of being spiritually reborn is the process of the gospel. It involves faith in Jesus Christ and complete repentance in order to undergo a mighty change. For "the holy scriptures...leadeth them to faith on the Lord, and unto repentance, which faith and repentance bringeth a change of heart unto them."[6]

As the father of King Lamoni asks, "what shall I do that I may be born of God?" Aaron answers his question: "If thou desirest this thing . . . if thou wilt repent of all thy sins, and will bow down before God, and call on his name in faith . . . then shalt thou receive the hope which thou desirest." So, the father of King Lamoni declares to God, "I will give away all my sins to know thee."[7] He goes unconscious, appearing to be dead, and then awakes born of God.

This spiritual rebirth transforms our desires as well as our behavior. Elder David A. Bednar provides a modern-day reminder: "This mighty change is not simply the result of working harder or developing greater individual discipline. Rather, it is the consequence of a fundamental change in our desires, our motives, and our natures . . . Our spiritual purpose is to overcome both sin and the desire to sin."[8]

Even after we experience a mighty change of heart,

maintaining that blessed state takes dedication and hard work. When our spirit and body get "out of alignment," emotionally, mentally, physically or spiritually, we feel ill at ease. That's when we're most likely to seek immediate relief in a variety of inappropriate ways and become tempted by unrighteous desires – often the same unrighteous desires we have struggled with before. We seek immediate relief in ways that can, with enough repetition, turn into bad habits or pernicious addictions. Then the natural man must be put off again in order to undergo another mighty change.

"But the natural man receiveth not the things of the Spirit of God: for they are foolishness unto him."[9]

"Therefore if any man be in Christ, he is a new creature: old things are passed away; behold, all things are become new."[10]

This powerful witness of change comes from the man who changed so dramatically that he was called by a new name, which represented his new identity. Saul was known as a persecutor of the disciples of Jesus Christ. After his mighty change on the road to Damascus, he became the great apostle, Paul. The change was so pronounced that later he boldly testified of the Savior, even while his own life was being threatened. "I am ready not to be bound only, but also to die at Jerusalem for the name of the Lord Jesus."[11]

Elder Bruce R. McConkie states: "there would be passions, appetites, and desires planted in the mortal body that were not there when we were in the preexistent sphere . . . Down here we're on probation as mortals, where appetites control our bodies, where we have lusts, and where we're subject to hunger, thirst, fatigue, disease, sexual appetites, and all the rest."[12]

Nature and nurture may influence us, but it is our divine nature that truly defines us, if we allow it to do so. We have the power to act rather than to be acted upon, becoming "agents" rather than "objects."[13] Our wayward desires do not have to take us off course, or keep us there. We determine the direction our lives will take.

Most importantly, our Savior, Jesus Christ, is the One who transforms our lives in ways we may not think humanly possible. And we may be right. It may not be humanly possible. President Benson reminds us: "The world would shape human behavior, but Christ can change human nature."[14]

In my first book, I emphasized how the healing power of the Atonement brought about a mighty change as it related to my homosexual attractions as well as my struggles with substance abuse. I describe those trials here, and include parts of my first book when telling my life story. I also discuss new challenges I've faced in the past two decades, like having a child with special needs.

By telling my story, I hope to show how spiritual rebirth enables us to overcome various manifestations of the natural man—from the negative effects of trials and circumstances to deliberate and addictive sinful behaviors.

This book is divided into four sections, encompassing mighty changes that have occurred in different ways at various times in my life. The first section is about my childhood, which is rather intense and disjointed. That's because my childhood memories are much like that—many experiences, all jumbled together, which have affected my life with such intensity, they've left indelible impressions. The other three sections are about leaving home, my temple marriage, and motherhood.

I have gained a greater understanding of what often lies beneath desires to sin, including such things as childhood trauma, emotional upheaval and distorted thinking. I've learned what helps facilitate growth, change, and healing from a psychological perspective by earning my master's degree in Mental Health Counseling, with an emphasis in addictions. My education, work, faith, and life experiences have combined to give me greater insights into how nature, nurture and the spirit create who we have been, who we are, and who we can become.

Sinful desires can be put off, in this life. In fact, that is precisely why we are here. Elder Bednar states, "The precise nature of the test of mortality, then, can be summarized in the following question: Will I respond to the inclinations of the natural man, or will I yield to the enticings of the Holy Spirit and put off the natural man and become a saint through the Atonement of Christ the Lord (see Mosiah 3:19)? That is the test. Every appetite, desire, propensity, and impulse of the natural man may be overcome by and through the Atonement of Jesus Christ. We are here on the earth to develop godlike qualities and to bridle all of the passions of the flesh."[15]

Through personal commitment to the gospel plan, hard work, and divine assistance, each one of us can live a life free from the grip of the natural man, regardless of how it has encumbered us. Whether we have struggled with fear or carelessness, financial loss or the love of money, unnecessary guilt or the rationalization of sins, a lack of self-esteem or an abundance of pride, anorexia or overeating, substance abuse or verbal abuse, viewing homosexual or heterosexual pornography, addiction to work or to video games. The list is endless. Fortunately, the Atonement is infinite.

We are all born into conditions of mortality, subjected to trials here on earth and asked to come off conqueror. All of us are born that way, in so many ways. It is Christ who asks us to become spiritually reborn–His Way.

{ Daughter of God }

MIGHTY CHANGE I

Keep a deep, dark secret long enough and it will start spreading on its own. Hidden misconceptions about childhood trauma grow from within, producing enough guilt and shame to squeeze the Light out of you. Even drag you down into your own personal gulf of misery and seemingly endless woe.

Yet, through Christ there can be healing. Mine is a story of redemption, to be sure. All that I am I owe to Jesus Christ and His saving grace.

My story is like so many others and not the same as anyone else's.

Having been abused as a child, I know how horrible and destructive it can be. I also know the strength and healing that can come, although a steep price must be paid.

Having grown up thinking I was gay and knowing I was Mormon, I have experienced the pain such conflict can bring. I also know the joy that can come from a temple marriage, yet some people with same-sex attractions talk about the wreckage left in its wake.

As far back as I can remember, I have had experiences that were extremely uplifting or extremely painful. Spiritual experiences or traumatic events. Faith or fear. Good or evil.

Life is a battle, after all. Not so much against "flesh and blood, but against principalities, against powers, against the rulers of the darkness of this world."[1]

When I was four years old, an evil witch would sneak into my dreams at night. She'd push my bed, with me in it, past my closet doors and into this huge, bottomless pit. As I spiraled downward, she would stare over the edge and laugh a wicked laugh.

In other dreams, ghostlike creatures would fly out from the attic door above our carport and swoop down at me as I tried to run out of our house. Sometimes I thought I saw ghosts or evil spirits when I was awake at night, often standing in my doorway. I'd hide under the covers or run full speed through the doorway, hoping to make it through the apparition and down the hall to my parents' bedroom.

As the nightmares and night time visits to my parents' bedroom continued, my mom came up with an inspired idea—the kind of idea that only a mother could come up with. She suggested we paint my closet doors with bright flowers, big butterflies, and a friendly, spirited frog to help keep the evil witch away.

It worked. That witch never returned, although sometimes the evil spirits would still chase me across my dreams and into the night.

I was deathly afraid of those nightmares. Yet, along with my fear—and it could be paralyzing at times—I remember my faith. I prayed for protection. I'd pray before I went to bed. I'd pray in bed when I couldn't sleep. I'd pray while I hid under the covers. I'd pray after a nightmare woke me up and before another one could begin.

I knew to whom I was praying. I can't remember ever *not* having a testimony of Jesus Christ and His restored gospel. My earliest childhood recollections include a strong sense of Heavenly Parents, an Elder Brother as my Savior, a heavenly home, and a lingering homesickness for heaven.

> *Yet oft-times, a secret something*
> *Whispered, "You're a stranger here,"*
> *And I felt that I had wandered*
> *From a more exalted sphere.* [2]

My sure knowledge of the Savior was not given to me by my earthly parents, although their tutoring was helpful and greatly appreciated. My knowledge was a gift from God. "To some it is given by the Holy Ghost to know that Jesus Christ is the Son of God, and that he was crucified for the sins of the world."[3] He who knows the beginning from the end was aware of how desperately I would need that testimony.

Born and Reborn.

I was born in 1960 and then born again several times after that. I can remember two of those times because they were so obvious and remarkable. The others were more gradual, making it tough to tell. Sort of like how it was for the Lamanites of Third Nephi who "were baptized with fire and with the Holy Ghost, and they knew it not."[4]

It's difficult because spiritual rebirth requires putting off the natural man, which can return as we're tempted to go back to our old ways.

I cannot afford to return to my old ways, nor do I want to. Although I don't always maintain a state of spiritual rebirth and I have to go through the process again and again, I have managed to abandon the most spiritually damaging parts of the natural man. It returns through other means now: fear and doubt, anxiety and depression, self-criticism and resentment, even sheer exhaustion.

Throughout my life, I've had many questions regarding the causes and effects of the "natural" part of me. Why did the abuse have to happen and mess me up so badly? Why did I desire lesbian relationships when the Lord forbids them? Why did I have to suffer with addictions when all I wanted was relief from the pain? Why would I have to be celibate the rest of my life in order to be faithful? (That question was partly answered later with a temple marriage.) Why did my depression and anxiety have to make it so difficult, even impossible at times, to feel the spirit and to be the kind of mother I wanted to be?

As I have matured in the gospel, I can look over my life and stop asking, "Why me?" Instead, I have learned to ask, "Why not me?" A good friend taught me that.

Sin City.

I was born and raised in Las Vegas, Nevada. My parents were both active Latter-day Saints who grew up in Utah as descendants of hardy pioneer stock. In 1957, my dad talked my mom into moving out to Las Vegas. That was back when Las Vegas consisted mostly of mobsters, burlesque girls, casinos, free buffets, barren deserts, a scorching sun, and a little-known family community that somehow managed to sprout up and then thrive in an inhospitable environment.

Just two blocks from our house was an elementary school with a huge playground and a Mormon church next door. On Tuesdays during lunch, my friends and I would walk over to church to have lunch with our moms during their weekly Relief Society gathering. They'd fix tuna fish or peanut butter and jelly sandwiches on Wonder Bread (no doubt hoping to "build strong bodies 12 ways"). We also had Jell-O and red punch, in keeping with fine Mormon tradition. Oh, how we loved Tuesdays.

The Mormons we met in other states found it hard to believe that faithful Latter-day Saints actually lived in Sin City. They seldom believed me when I told them Mormons helped settle the place in the late 1800s. In fact, the Old Las Vegas Mormon Fort still stands today, just a coin's toss away from the huddled mass of casinos that make up downtown Fremont Street.

I assumed we lived in a town like the one on *Leave it to Beaver*. Our parents loved us and graciously fulfilled their parental duties. The homes in our neighborhood were small but nice, with neatly cropped lawns and hedges. We played hopscotch, jump rope, kickball, foursquare, hide and go seek, and whatever games we could create in our neighbor's swimming pool to help battle the summer heat.

Some of the differences are more obvious in hindsight. We had a mini craps table and roulette wheel at home. Poker was my favorite card game, using the chips from our Tripoli game. I could bluff with the best of 'em. Also, my great aunt had a slot machine in her basement and whenever we went to visit, we'd race down the stairs calling "first dibs" in a hotly debatable order.

I don't suppose Mormons in other towns spent a few family home evenings driving up and down Fremont Street. It never ceased to amaze me how that place always looked bright as day, especially after the sun went down. Massive bulb-studded signs lined the street and stretched into the skyline. They seemed especially gargantuan to us kids. Like the boulder-sized, glittering Golden Nugget, the Silver Slipper big enough for a giant princess, and, my favorite, the thumb's-up, arm-waving Howdy Partner cowboy that towered above the Pioneer Club.

Vegas residents always said you never really noticed downtown and the Strip. We had a little of it right in our neighborhood, however, because a burlesque dancer was our next-door neighbor. She liked to garden and work in the front yard wearing a G-string on the bottom and pasties on top, so tan lines wouldn't ruin her work, I suppose. Whenever a neighborhood mom would complain, she'd politely go inside and come back out wearing just a little bit more. I remember commenting to Mom that I didn't understand all the fuss since there wasn't much difference between our neighbor and the topless ladies from Africa in our National Geographic Magazines.

I loved that there were slot machines by the front door at Macayo Vegas, my favorite Mexican restaurant. Whenever we'd have to wait to be seated or pay the check, Dad would pass me a few nickels. I'd slip them into the machine and pull down on the handle as hard as I could. That fun ended the day I hit the jackpot. A loud bell started ringing as the nickels cascaded down, clanging into the metal tray below. I started scooping up the nickels just before Dad scooped me up and rushed me outside.

"Dad, I didn't get all the nickels!"

He shushed me with the loudest shush I'd ever heard. "You weren't supposed to hit the jackpot!"

I looked back at him, puzzled. I'd always figured that hitting the jackpot was the goal. Apparently not. Mom came out, unhappy with both of us.

Dad always bent or broke the rules and it would upset Mom. Sometimes it was funny. Other times it got ugly. I hated it when my parents argued. I also hated to disappoint either one of them. I always tried very hard to do the right thing, or at least what I thought was right.

Long after I hit that jackpot, and missed the spoils, Mom kept me close to her side whenever we had to wait for a table or linger near slot machines (except for the one in Aunt Venice's basement, of course).

One of my dad's favorite Las Vegas stories took place when he went to a land auction in the early 1960s. He wanted to purchase a few acres as an investment. The front row was filled with men in fancy dark suits. Dad said everybody there knew they were from the mafia, so no one dared bid against them. Dad and the rest of the civilians sat there, silently, not moving a muscle or a paddle while "the boys" purchased much of the south end of the Las Vegas strip–all for about $300 an acre. After they were finished, my dad managed to purchase three acres out in the boonies. A casino is on that land now, too.

I was never really sure how either one of my parents felt about the gospel. I don't know why I wondered about their testimonies, but I did. They lived most commandments, as near as I could tell. I just remember having this sense that I felt strongly about the gospel and my parents seemed more casual about it. I wasn't sure how my older brothers and sister felt, either. Maybe that's because we never really talked about our testimonies.

Etched in my soul is one particular afternoon when we were walking home from sacrament meeting. I was six or seven years old. I spotted a bright green praying mantis straddling the red pyracantha berries. As the family went on ahead, I examined the scene more closely. I often lagged behind, stopping to look, touch and examine everything more closely, taking in nature and the world around me.

I picked up the praying mantis and held him up at eye level, and then stared into his big round bug eyes. I figured I'd won the staring contest when he turned his head (the only insect that can do that). I watched him as he jumped into a magnificent sky.

It was late afternoon and rays of sunlight were shining through the clouds, separating into distinct lines that shot out toward the ground. I'd never seen a sky quite like that before. I was sure it was just how the sky would look when Christ came again.

I began to sing, "I wonder when He comes again."[5] I did not wonder *if* Christ would come again, only *when*. I would not have been surprised if He had returned that afternoon. In fact, I stood there watching the heavens and waiting for a little while, just in case.

Baptism by water and by fire.

I clearly remember how excited I was to finally turn eight because it meant I could get baptized. I'd stolen Silly Putty from the store in second grade and even smoked a couple of cigarette butts off the sidewalk with some friends. (It was just as nasty as it sounds.) Although I'd repented at least a million times, I was convinced I could not be completely forgiven of my "serious sins" until I was washed clean through baptism.

I was baptized at the old Las Vegas Stake Center, which later became the Reed Whipple Center (there was only one stake in Vegas at the time). I can still picture my dad standing in the font, holding out his hands to help me down. After he prayed and immersed me in the cold water, I stood back up, having been washed clean. It was an amazing feeling. I truly felt clean. The confirmation was powerful, too. I had the very real sense that I'd received the gift of the Holy Ghost, a baptism by fire. I was truly born again.

In the days and weeks that followed, I paid attention to how I felt. I wanted to recognize the influence of the Holy Ghost. Even though I didn't hear a voice, I did notice that I had certain impressions or ideas about things I should do and things I shouldn't do. I had always been inclined to choose the right, but making the decision to do so seemed easier somehow. It was like I had help. Like I had Jiminy Cricket, I figured.

I was intent on being a righteous new member of The Church of Jesus Christ of Latter-day Saints. That was the most important thing in my life at the time.

{ 19 }

Measuring the waters and weighing the mountains.

Suzie was my best friend growing up. She lived just down the street from us. Oh, how I loved playing at her house. She had six brothers and sisters, and that seemed like two or three more kids than her mom could keep track of. Their house was always a mess. A huge, glorious mess. The kind of mess a kid like me could only dream of. After all, our house was consistently spotless, making it much less fun and a lot more work.

Suzie's chemistry set was my very favorite toy. That was back before lawsuits were all the rage, so it had all sorts of exciting (and hazardous) contents. There were at least 20 different chemicals and compounds, various test tubes, pipettes, funnels, rubbing alcohol, litmus paper, steel wool and a Bunsen burner. A recipe for disaster, when unsupervised kids are added. Fortunately, neither of us ever got seriously hurt. Unless you count the time that Suzie got a spanking as the result of one of our chemistry experiments gone awry.

We mixed a bunch of chemicals together, put them in the street, and then poured some alcohol on top, for good measure. I lit a match and threw it on the pile, just before a neighbor came driving around the corner. Apparently she didn't appreciate driving through our pyrotechnic display, and she let Suzie's mom know about it.

Of all the chemicals, I liked sulphur the best. We'd mix it up with whatever liquids were handy, heat it up, and watch it go from a solid to a liquid to a gas. It would bubble up and release the strong scent of Yellowstone. Suzie hated the rotten egg smell, but I loved it. The smell reminded me of the trips our family took to Yellowstone. Bubbling mud pots, spouting geysers, clouds of sulphur-laden steam. All very rudimentary, earth-in-the-making sort of stuff.

I've always been curious about how the earth was made. What was it like during its formative years? Were we there? Did we really help?

Every jagged rock or exposed cliff piques the imagination. I remember hiking down through Queen's Garden in Bryce Canyon and mingling with the rock formations. Even their name is intriguing – the hoodoos. I would run my hand across the siltstone and limestone layers, reaching up as high as I possibly could.

Did Christ, or someone else, plan how each spire would take shape? Were there rough sketches or scale models? Was sand dripped, like with sand castles at the beach, to make miniature replicas? Were the deep orange and red of the rock placed against various backdrops, like a bright blue sky or an orange and purple sunset?

In some distant place beyond time, maybe we'll take classes to learn how to do it ourselves. Or, perhaps we've already taken them and a veil shrouds what we learned.

I can just imagine taking a class like Canyon Building 101. Materials list includes the following: All elements from the periodic table. Plenty of sand, gravel, silt, fire and ice. Rain, snow, frost and lightning. Mix ingredients as demonstrated. Add extra manganese, iron and copper for desired colors. Bring to a rolling boil and spread out in layers. Let harden while mixing additional ingredients. Break layers from beneath and force upward. Repeat. Repeat. Repeat. Centrifuge slowly. Use forced air and water to shape.

The lab would likely be filled with familiar odors – damp

soil, fresh rain, sulphur, iron, moss, and sunshine. Someone would probably get caught messing around with the quicksand, or heating up enough sulphur to get the whole place smelling like rotten eggs.

It must have been magnificent to watch the Creator at work, the Master Teacher. He who "measured the waters in the hollow of his hand, and meted out heaven with the span, and comprehended the dust of the earth in a measure, and weighed the mountains in scales, and the hills in a balance".[6]

I hope I'm registered for classes.

A youngster's sacred prayer in a grove of trees.

My fascination with nature was ignited and frequently rekindled by the many family vacations we took in our Ford station wagon. From camping in remote, out-of-the-way places that Dad could always find to visiting famous national parks – back when they were filled with natural wonders rather than busloads of tourists.

Dad brought along our well-worn Rand McNally maps. Scenic roads were marked in blue, and we'd follow one whenever we got the chance. It was called blue roading – the longest, most spectacular way to get anywhere.

Sometimes you could tell how amazing a blue road might be just by the name. Like the Blue Ridge Parkway that chases spectacular views of the evergreen-draped Blue Ridge Mountains as they turn various shades of blue and disappear across the horizon. Or the Avenue of the Giants, winding its way through the mighty redwoods of Northern California.

Occasionally the name was deceiving. Like Schnebley

Road that heads out behind Sedona, Arizona, and takes you through twisted red rock formations that cradle the town nature painted red.

Our family vacations were a blessing from my parents. I'm so grateful that they sacrificed their time and went to all the effort required to take a family of six on vacation. Nature helped build a strong spiritual foundation for me. Over the years, it has helped me feel the Spirit in ways that have proven to be an integral part of my soul and spiritual development. Nature is a place of communion with the Holy Spirit and the Father of all Creation.

At the beginning of the summer just after I turned ten, our family went on a particularly grand adventure. We left the West in our station wagon piled high with luggage and toting a canvas desert water bag in front, just in case the radiator got any wild notions. It was to be a long, hot drive. Unfortunately, those of us in the back seats couldn't feel any air conditioning because the only air vents in those days were on the front dashboard. So, my dad cut a long strip of plastic from a dry cleaning bag and taped it lengthwise to form a makeshift air duct that was about the size of a softball in circumference. He taped one of the ends of the tube around the main air conditioning vent on the dashboard and then ran the tube to the back seat. He put tape from the tube up to the roof of the car to hold it in place.

It looked like a miniature version of the exposed air conditioning ductwork you find in a warehouse or loft. All we knew was that the open end of that tube was worth fighting for because you could point the cool air right at your face.

We drove all over the United States and did all sorts of things. We visited an Amish community, a Ford assembly line, the Kellogg's cereal plant, Kitty Hawk, Mt. Rushmore, Williamsburg, Gettysburg, Statue of Liberty, Empire State Building, Smithsonian Institute, and the Jefferson, Washington and Lincoln Memorials, to name a few.

I saw fireflies for the first time when we camped on the shore of a small scenic lake in Wisconsin. I caught them in a jar that soon glowed like a lantern. I got soaking wet from the overspray at Niagara Falls and tasted maple syrup fresh from the maple trees in Vermont. We drove clear up to Maine, just across the state line where Dad pulled over. He opened the car door, stuck his foot out onto the ground, brought it back into the car, closed the door and turned the car back around, heading south through New Hampshire. Maine was the last of the 50 United States Dad had left to visit. He said he wanted to be able to brag that he'd set foot in all 50 states. He literally set his foot in Maine, and that was it. None of the rest of us even touched ground in Maine. I always sort of liked it that way because it was a great story to tell my friends.

We also visited LDS historic sites on that trip, which included Carthage Jail, Nauvoo, and the Sacred Grove.

Of all the places we visited on our grand vacation, of all the incredible natural and man-made wonders, what impressed me the most was a small grove of trees in upstate New York. As soon as I entered the Sacred Grove, I felt the spirit. There was so much "evidence of things not seen."[7] Evidence of a young boy kneeling in prayer, the Father and the Son appearing to him, and the restoration of the gospel that formed the very essence of my being.

My family and I were the only ones in the grove that morning. I wandered off to find where I thought Joseph had knelt in prayer. I came to an area that had a group of trees that were smaller than the surrounding ones. I was certain it must have been the clearing where Joseph prayed. So, I knelt in prayer and proclaimed my testimony of the gospel, of Joseph Smith and the Father and Son who appeared to him, of the golden plates that he translated, and of all the modern-day prophets who have followed.

My life was permanently anchored and my testimony sealed that morning. All with the humble prayer of a ten-year-old girl in a small grove of trees in upstate New York.

"God loves me, God loves me not?"

A month and a half after our marvelous cross-country adventure, I took a trip that was as far to the other extreme as a ten-year-old can get. It left me feeling that God was disgusted with me and might not ever love me again.

I went to visit Chad and Shelly, our family friends who owned a small farm in northern Nevada. I was so excited to visit a real farm. Plus, it was the first time I got to take a trip by myself and fly on an airplane.

An airline stewardess accompanied me. I thought I was the only person special enough to receive a personal escort. From my window seat, I had a close-up view of the world. The men putting baggage on a moving ramp, our plane slowly rolling forward while other planes rolled ahead and behind—like we were in a slow motion race. Then, as the runway began to fly faster and faster beneath us, I watched in amazement as we lifted up off the ground. People soon turned to matchsticks, the cars to bugs, and the streets to ant trails. I looked for our house across the vast landscape of miniature roofs, swimming pools and parks. When we climbed above the big billowy clouds, it looked as if I could step off the wing and bounce alongside the plane.

My first two days of life on a farm were equally new and exciting. Not only did I ride a horse, I rode one bareback. I learned how to operate a tractor. I played with the chickens and slopped around with the pigs.

On the third day, however, farm life and my life took a horrible turn.

It became time to "prepare" a few of the chickens. I hadn't made the connection that the chickens we'd been eating came from the same coop as the chickens I'd been naming and playing with. I was fine with the eggs. I would collect them from the chickens in the mornings and we'd scramble them up for breakfast. But the chickens were different. They were *live* animals.

I went outside and threw some feed on the ground as I called the chickens, a few by name, and they gathered round. No one ever told me the cardinal rule of farming: never name the animals.

Chad came out of the house and started walking toward us. The chickens scattered, like they knew something I didn't. Suddenly, Chad lunged at them and came up with his fist clenched tightly around Ping's neck. Ping was a special chicken. I'd named her after *The Story About Ping*, one of my favorite children's books.

Before I could say anything or react, Chad slammed

Ping down onto a large wooden stump and stretched her neck over the edge. Then he raised an axe that he'd kept hidden at his side. With a steady swing that spoke volumes of his experience in such matters, his axe struck the chopping block and Ping went flying.

It all happened so fast, I wasn't sure what he'd done. (It's amazing how many traumatic events occur in the time it takes to swing an axe.) Ping started flapping her wings in a feathered fury, spraying blood all over.

She flew straight over me, squirting blood across my face and chest. Then she rolled a few times as she landed on the other side of the wooden fence. By the time I got to her, she was jerking around in a slop of dirt and blood. While still hoping to help, I rolled her over. That was when I finally noticed her head was missing.

I stiffened up and stared wide-eyed as blood shot out from where her head used to be. The blood squirted all over me. There was blood everywhere. I'd never seen so much blood in my life.

As I held the bloody, flapping, headless chicken-turned-pet-turned-dinner, Chad walked up to me, quite matter-of-factly, and said, "Put it down. It'll bleed out."

I stared up with a horrified look on my bloodied face.

"C'mon kid," he insisted. "Go get cleaned up. You got blood all over you."

He grabbed my arm and yanked me up, not very carefully. "Don't worry. That chicken never knew what hit 'er."

That was the first and last time I ever named a farm animal. However, that was not the traumatic event that changed my life forever. It happened later that day.

{ 27 }

Shelly took their three-year-old into town to do some grocery shopping. I stayed home and watched TV with Chad. A little while after they left, he asked me if I wanted to go get an ice cream cone. Of course I did. Excitedly, I jumped into his car with visions of Rocky Road ice cream dancing in my head.

Tragically, that wasn't what Chad had on his mind.

He drove us down a dirt road that ran through some farmland and then parked behind a small group of trees. He told me to get into the back seat. Then he climbed on top of me as my neck stretched across the edge of the seat.

It didn't take him much longer than the swing of an axe to traumatize my life.

When he was finished, we drove back to the house. I stared wide-eyed without saying a word the whole way.

My childhood had fallen beneath the hot, sticky seat of a '62 Chevy. Lost forever, like a precious coin.

I didn't gather eggs the next morning. I stayed out of the house and wandered around in the backyard, mostly in a state of shock. When Chad came out to talk, I clutched the clothesline pole as if a twister were about to strike.

It did.

"If you tell my wife or your parents what happened, you'll be in big trouble. You never told me 'no,' remember? You know you wanted it."

Oh, how that twisted phrase would warp my life: "You never said no."

I believed that it was my fault. Ten-year-olds have no idea how pedophiles twist and destroy the truth in order to cover their trail of carnage.

His wife drove me to the airport when it was time to go home. I was just as quiet as an obedient child should be. A stewardess escorted me to the plane, I suppose. All I really remember about the trip back home to Las Vegas was staring blankly out the window at the cars and streets, deserts and mountains and clouds. I might as well have been staring at a brick wall.

I did not tell his wife.

I did not tell my parents.

I did not tell a soul.

Silence is the slow torture of abuse.

Guilt and its warp factor.

I was 12 years old when a friend came over to tell me she'd heard sex was the worst sin next to murder and you could get kicked out of the Church. Suddenly, I realized just what Chad meant when he said I shouldn't tell anyone about the awful thing I'd done. No wonder I shouldn't tell. I'd get kicked out of the Church. The Church that meant everything to me.

The following year, I received a diary for Christmas. It was my very first journal. I wanted to write all about how guilty I felt – for that was the only real feeling I had – but I was afraid that somebody might read it. In lieu of a full confession, I decided to etch a small "g" in the upper right-hand corner of the page corresponding to the days I felt guilty. After three months, I could not bear to write in my diary any longer. Every single page had a "g" in the upper right-hand corner. I threw the journal away, but day after day continued, just like the turning of pages, each bearing the mark of "guilty."

I worked hard to cover my guilt and act like nothing was wrong. I got good grades, had plenty of friends, served faithfully in Church callings and played sports. All the while I was convinced that Heavenly Father was disgusted with me, and everyone else would be, too, if only they knew who I really was and what I'd done.

As my faith in the gospel continued to increase, so did my belief that I was a horrible person. Chad had convinced me that I'd done something terribly wrong and it was my fault. Yet, all I'd ever wanted to do was the right thing. I even had a CTR ring to prove it.

The aftermath of the molestation was tragic. I winced and cowered in shame every time we had a chastity lesson at church: in seminary, Sunday School, youth group meetings, firesides, and camp. The lessons seemed to come from every direction in rapid-fire succession.

That was back in the day when no one imagined that good kids from strong, church-going families could ever be the victims of sexual abuse.

Those well-intentioned, yet misguided, church lessons took their toll. A terrible, secret toll I kept hidden beneath my Sunday best. The only one I couldn't hide from was me. And those incessant lessons.

"If you commit a sexual sin, you'll never be the same. Lost virginity can never be found."

"Sinning is like pounding nails in a board. You can take out the nails by repenting, but the holes are still there."

"Which would you rather have, a new car or a used one?"

The lesson I remember most was the one in which my teacher used a fresh carnation to drive the point home. He gave the carnation to the first student in the front row and told him to examine it and pass it on. I was sitting in the last seat on the back row and ended up with this poor, dilapidated carnation that everyone had manhandled.

"See," the teacher said, "if you break the law of chastity, you'll end up like that poor carnation."

I wilted in my chair.

I mistakenly thought I'd broken the law of chastity. In reality, Chad was the one who had broken the law, which, in turn, broke me.

I emerged from childhood with a fractured soul.

It got to the point where not only did chastity lessons bother me, but so did any mention of procrastinating the day of repentance. I was convinced I needed to "confess" my supposed sexual sins to my bishop. I just kept putting it off because I was sure I'd be excommunicated and my whole life would be ruined.

As the tension continued to build inside of me, a little green book pushed me to the breaking point.

In a Young Women's class, we were given a small book by Spencer W. Kimball titled *Hidden Wedges*. After reading it, I began feeling worse about my supposed grievous sins and the procrastination of my confession to the bishop.

It never occurred to me that I didn't need to confess, although I desperately needed to tell someone in order to get help. Unfortunately, I didn't think I deserved any help. Only punishment.

Spencer W. Kimball wrote *Hidden Wedges* when he

was an apostle, after he'd had a week filled with people coming to see him "in anguish of soul; folks learning repentance through life's penalties... in spiritual deficiencies... they had forgotten promises and covenants, procrastinating their repentance."[8] It reminded him of Samuel T. Whitman's *Forgotten Wedges*.

The story of the wedge began when a farmer was a young boy on his father's homestead. He was splitting logs and set the wedge between the limbs of a young walnut tree when he ran to dinner, thinking he'd retrieve it later. He never did. The tree grew around the wedge as it matured into a large, beautiful tree.

One day an ice storm hit. As ice collected on the tree, the weight became too much, and one of the three major limbs broke off the trunk where the wedge had been placed years before. This unbalanced the rest of the tree, so it split apart and crashed to the ground.

"Forgotten wedges! Hidden weaknesses grown over and invisible, waiting until some winter night to work their ruin. What better symbolizes the presence and the effect of sin."

He continues, "The life we prized so much goes down in the unspeakable loss of spiritual disaster." In the end, "a fallen tree, split and shattered and worthless."[9]

That little green book gave words–the words of an apostle and prophet, no less–to my own misperceptions. I was fallen, split, shattered and worthless. I thought the hidden wedge was my "sexual indiscretion."

In actuality, the hidden wedge was the abuse that had been forced on me and the shame that unduly ensued.

The shame experienced by abused children can be as

devastating as the act of abuse itself. A child often accepts the abuser's words as truth and takes on his perversions as her own. The twisted, broken events and misperceptions form a twisted, broken sense of self.

Over time, the guilt became too heavy for me to bear. I began to crack under the weight and seriously considered suicide. Eventually, I decided suicide would be worse than the sin I'd already committed.

In desperation, I prayed to my Heavenly Father, asking whether or not I should talk to the bishop.

"Yes."

The response startled me. It was my very first, and only, audible answer I've ever received to a prayer.

So, I went in and "confessed" to the bishop. It did not occur to me that I was not at fault and that there was nothing for which I needed to confess. Unfortunately, my bishop didn't know how to handle a victim of sexual abuse. At the time, bishops had no pamphlets, referral systems, or helplines for assistance like they have now.

The bishop simply asked me whether or not I realized what I did was wrong. Then he asked me if the man had penetrated me. I didn't even know what that meant.

That was pretty much the extent of it. There was no recognition that I had been a young girl who was victimized. I received no reassurance of my innocence. I left the bishop's office relieved that I had kept my Church membership but profoundly disappointed that I'd kept most of the guilt.

The gap continued to widen between the awful sinner I thought I was and the perfect person I worked so hard to present to the world.

For time and not always eternity.

Although my parents were fine when they were apart, their arguing continued with more frequency when they were together. Dad was a risk taker. Mom was cautious. Dad would take us on exciting, sometimes dangerous adventures. Mom wanted to keep us safe and everything else in its perfect frame: a spotless home, as in no dirt, dust, spilled milk, misplaced shoes, dirty dishes, unmade beds, or unraked carpet. (I hated raking our long shag carpet. "Why do I have to rake the carpet? None of my friends have to rake carpet!")

Our avocado green GE side-by-side refrigerator was the Gaza Strip of our household. Nothing got my mother's dander up faster than fingerprints on the refrigerator. Mom figured it should be under her control because she did all the grocery shopping, cooking, and cleaning. Dad claimed it as his territory because he liked to snack and he felt like he had paid for the food. And for the refrigerator.

Mom kept it clean, inside and out. Dad messed it up, inside and out. Every day, Mom would wipe off the front of the fridge, keeping it shiny like a beloved sports car. (It was her version of one, I suppose.) Every day, Dad would open the refrigerator door, place his left hand high on the closed freezer half, and lean into the fridge as he slowly examined and re-examined each shelf of food.

Mom could always tell when Dad had been resting his hand on the freezer because it left a faint, oily print. At least, she said it did. I couldn't see it. She'd point to the top of the fridge in disgust and Dad would stare back, as if he were innocent. Mom would throw a fit and then Dad would throw one back at her.

I fully expected to come home one day and find that Dad had put his hands in dirty motor oil and then plastered his handprints all over the fridge. In retaliation, Mom would put a lock and chain on the refrigerator so Dad couldn't get any food out, ever again.

It wasn't the refrigerator that did the marriage in, however. My mother would say that it was the M-80 explosion that blasted it apart.

We used to love M-80s at our house. They're those little cardboard tubes about the size of a shotgun shell, containing 5 grams of explosives with a fuse sticking out the side. Dad would take us out on bombing raids, usually up at our family cabin in central Utah. He'd stick one in a beaver dam and we'd watch the water blow sky high, with sticks and logs shooting off in all directions. Or, he'd bury one in a riverbank so we could watch the mud fly.

One time my brothers and I collected a bunch of cow patties from the meadow (crispy as well as fresh) and put them in a big pile on top of a piece of cardboard. Dad lifted the cardboard up slightly and put the M-80 under it. After he lit the fuse, we all took off running in different directions. It didn't matter who ran the fastest, though, because none of us escaped the cow pie meteor shower. You could hear it splatter all over us as we screeched under the barrage of fresh manure.

We had manure in our hair and all over our clothes. We stank to high-heaven as we walked back to the cabin, late for dinner. Mom's a great cook, and the delicious supper she'd prepared for us had grown cold.

You-know-what hit the fan.

But the M-80 explosion to end all explosions happened on a family picnic. Dad decided to startle us by secretly throwing an M-80 into the creek by our picnic table. He lit what turned out to be a quick fuse. He noticed it and let go just as it exploded.

I was standing nearby and got splattered with what I thought was mud. Looking closely, I realized it was blood. I thought it might be my own, but I didn't hurt anywhere. Then Dad let out a horrifying sound I'd never heard from him before. I looked over to see him clutching a bloody mass at the end of his right arm and running toward the creek. I ran after him and got there just as he pulled his injured hand back out of the creek.

For a split second, before the blood rushed back out again, I could see the bones in two of his fingers.

I didn't know what to do and I froze. Fortunately, the rest of the family wasn't too far behind me.

All I could think to do was rinse Dad's blood off my jacket, slowly and rather methodically. I continued to feel frozen in place. I was probably in a mild state of shock, being taken back in an instant to when I was splattered with Ping's blood and then the abuse that followed.

Trauma has a way of piling up in the same place in your brain. Then the pile comes back at you with full force. Like it's all happening again, all at once. When you experience another trauma or something that reminds you of one, it adds to the pile. In fact, they have found that the soldiers who are most likely to suffer from Post-Traumatic Stress Disorder (PTSD) are those who have experienced trauma in their childhood.[10]

Somehow they got Dad's hand stitched back together, although it required several grafts. Two of his fingers never looked quite right. He was out of work and stuck at home for three months, and taking pain medication. That's when the problems at home seemed to escalate.

My mom sees the M-80 incident as the turning point in their marriage. I felt like their marriage was doomed long before that. At any rate, the decline of my parents' marriage really gained momentum from there on out.

Less than a year after the M-80 explosion, my mom warned me that a divorce was imminent. She was trying to prepare me for the tumult. I can't imagine there is any way a kid can prepare for something like that.

A few months later, I came home from school and saw that Dad's car and motorcycle were both gone. I ran to my parents' room and noticed that the TV was missing. In a frenzy, I ran to my dad's closet and flung open the doors. The closet was empty, except for a few hangers and an old pair of suspenders–the suspenders he wore on his waders when he took me fishing.

I threw myself against the back of the closet and slid down to the floor. I sat there wishing I could cry, but Dad didn't believe in crying.

I came to the very harsh realization that families are not always forever.

Later that day, Dad came home to talk to me about the breakup. He told me he'd tried to make the marriage last, that he had wanted to stay until I'd graduated from high school, but he just couldn't do it. Then he started to sob. The man who taught me to take everything on the chin was crying. I'd never seen him shed a single tear in his life.

I hugged him and told him everything was going to be okay. Then I felt myself going numb again, like with Ping and Chad and the rapid-fire chastity lessons and the M-80.

I wished it were me crying and Dad who was holding me. I always knew Dad loved me. I never doubted it, or my love for him. Yet, there he was, finally opening up to me and showing true emotion, just as he was walking out the door.

From the moment Dad left, it never felt like home again.

I didn't even know parents could get a divorce if they'd been sealed in the temple. I thought that meant they were married for time and all eternity. No other Mormon family we knew had ever split up. That really wasn't happening much back in the 1970s.

My friends and church leaders didn't know how to react or what to say to me. I didn't know what to say, either, so nothing was said at all. That added to my sense of isolation.

One Sunday, months after the divorce, Dad agreed to come to church with me. When we walked in, a hush fell over the back row. One of my Young Women leaders made a point of glaring at Dad, and then looking away in disgust. At the Young Women lessons she taught after that, her Christian comments felt hypocritical.

It seemed like everything was changing, for the worse.

Our household quickly went from one of contention to one of depression. I hated to spend any time there because it didn't feel like home. All I could really see was a ghost of a family, memories of good times past, and my deep longing to go back to life as it once was.

I didn't simply want to go back before the divorce. I

wanted to go clear back before the sexual abuse, and before Mom and Dad fought all the time. Back to when I found wonder in the smell of sulphur and spouting geysers, a praying mantis that could turn its head, and rays of sun that came straight from heaven.

I am sure I knew, logically, that there was no going back. But that didn't matter. It didn't stop my longing for it. And my homesickness for heaven made matters worse.

The divorce dealt Mom a heavy blow, too. She had a tough time just getting out of bed every day. Whenever she reached out to me, I refused to have anything to do with her because my own ship was sinking. I figured it was every woman for herself. Besides, I couldn't stand to go into her bedroom, the one she used to share with Dad. Half the bed was empty. Half the closet was empty. And I felt completely empty. I felt trapped where I didn't want to be – physically, emotionally or spiritually.

It would have been smart for me to open up to my older brother who was still at home. We were both suffering a great deal from the aftermath of the divorce. Unfortunately, I didn't talk to him much. He started hanging out at a friend's house to escape. I started hanging out at my sister's house for support. She had gotten married and moved back to Las Vegas with her husband. I started spending as much time as I could over there. She and her husband were both really good to me. It was a huge blessing, especially because my sister was the one person I could talk to about our parents' divorce. It didn't hit her as hard because she was out of the house by then. But the divorce was tough on her, too.

Divorce is tough on everyone.

Forbidden attractions.

My attraction toward girls started to manifest itself as my whole world fell apart. I didn't act on anything because of my testimony. I was helped by the fact that most of my attractions were focused on someone I couldn't have – an assistant softball coach who was a recent college graduate. I knew she was a lesbian and that she had a partner, but that didn't stop me from fantasizing about her and wishing we could be together. I envied the fact that she was old enough to live on her own, too. I found that to be every bit as attractive as she was.

I didn't really think my same-sex attractions were all that strange because I had several friends who liked other girls. I think one of them was interested in me. She probably refrained from doing something about it because I wasn't interested in anything more than a friendship. Not to mention, I was secretly in love with the assistant coach.

Looking back, I think that it may have been the coach's unavailability that was part of the attraction. After all, I had a strong testimony of the gospel and couldn't foresee ever acting on those feelings.

Like most of the young people who experience same-sex attraction, I didn't choose to have those feelings. I had no idea where they came from. Many LDS youth, and others, feel extremely guilty for having such attractions. I felt guilty for having them, but I figured thinking about them was better than acting on them. I still felt so much guilt from the sexual abuse for which I blamed myself. "Having sex with a man" seemed like more of a sin than wanting to be with a woman. Still, both of them added to my personal conviction that I was somehow flawed.

I was helped by the fact that, back then, there was little insistence that having gay feelings meant you were gay and that you had no choice in the matter. I assumed I'd have more choices in the future.

Regardless, my same-sex attraction was yet another cause of guilt, shame, secrecy, isolation and pain.

More hidden wedges.

As all of those negative feelings increased, I began to distance myself from the Church. It was just too painful. I didn't like how some Mormons shunned my father and spoke of him in unchristian terms. I hated the derogatory comments and distasteful jokes about gays. The attitudes of some members added to the sense that I didn't belong.

Alcohol came on the scene right about then. Several of my friends in high school drank. I went to some parties but did not imbibe. I never felt any peer pressure to join them. Sometimes they'd joke, in fun, because I was Mormon. And they spiked my 7-Up once, thinking they were so clever. They poured so much alcohol in my cup that it smelled to high heaven. Drunken people aren't very good at putting one over on a sober person.

One thing did intrigue me about drinking though, and it had nothing to do with fitting in. What I was drawn to most was how my friends seemed to be so carefree when they were drunk. I remember thinking how nice it would be to just quit worrying about everything—the guilt, the self-loathing, the secrets and isolation, my parents' divorce, my lack of anything that felt like home, the attraction to my coach, and on and on. The idea of having the weight of my world lifted, even if it were just for a brief moment, became increasingly appealing.

Eventually, I made plans to get drunk with a friend of mine. I knew she had access to her parents' liquor cabinet. She sneaked a bottle of rum and we bought a bottle of Coke. Not knowing what we were doing, we mixed it half and half. The combination was the worst thing I'd ever tasted in my life. But that did not deter me. I was on a mission to get drunk, as quickly as possible.

It didn't take long before I started to feel the effects. My often-anxious breathing began to slow. The tenseness in my arms and chest eased up. The rest of my hypervigilance began to fade as I no longer felt the need to maintain my false self in order to hide my presumably "evil self." It felt as though I were being relieved of duty, finally.

The guilt began to disappear, too. I didn't feel bad about myself or my attractions. I quit worrying that I had committed the worst sin next to murder, and that I'd go to hell for it. I quit worrying about my feelings for the assistant coach. I didn't feel the deep hole in my soul left by my parents' divorce. I didn't feel the darkness and the depression.

I just didn't feel, and that was the best feeling of all.

Of course, the relief didn't last long. I soon decided that since a little rum had done me so much good, then more rum would be even better. So, I started chugging straight from the bottle. My friend told me to slow down. I told her I'd be just fine. And I was, until my head started spinning and my stomach started churning.

I had to lie down on the ground as everything started

spinning around. Even the ground started spinning. Then I got sick and lost most of the rum.

The next day, I felt sicker than I had the night before. Far worse than the hangover, which was certainly bad, was the spiritual sickness. It was the first time I'd ever broken the Word of Wisdom (not counting the time I smoked the cigarette butts off the ground, of course). So, I had to add getting drunk to my large, soul-breaking load of heavy burdens that I carried around.

Even with the hangover and the guilt unto repentance and beyond, I was left with the very distinct and indelible impression that there was something that could relieve my pain. It was forbidden by the Lord, to be sure. But spending just a couple of precious hours guilt-free and pain-free was something I would not soon forget. There was even a sense of peace—albeit counterfeit peace—because all the turmoil seemed to disappear.

The feelings of relief that were facilitated by the alcohol reached deep into that same place where all of the trauma lived. It left its mark in there as a protection and a solution that later served as a huge stumbling block for my sobriety.

My need for relief and for peace were spiritual needs. Unfortunately, I wasn't filling them correctly. Just because needs are righteous, that doesn't necessarily mean they're being met in righteous ways.

As Elder Neal A. Maxwell states: "Sin, for instance, is often the wrongheaded ... way of expressing some basic needs that we all have, such as belonging and recognition. The adversary understands and plays upon these basic needs."[11]

Many alcoholics report they remember well the first

time they got drunk and that they immediately felt some relief and/or elation–as if they had found a remedy to a malady they can't explain. That speaks to the importance of avoiding even one drink. Otherwise, it's welcome to the world of Satan's counterfeits. And it can be hell trying to get out of there. I bear witness of that.

My favorite AA quote is "One drink is too many for me and a thousand not enough."[12]

"Dews from heaven."

I could tell he'd entered the room before I even turned around. The spirit distilled upon my "soul as the dews from heaven."[13] I turned to see President Spencer W. Kimball walking up the aisle of our stake center.

The opening song was "We Thank Thee, O God, For a Prophet." It was difficult for me to sing the words as I was gripped by the power and the tenderness of the moment. I was, indeed, filled with thankfulness to God "for a prophet to guide us in these latter days."[14]

I wasn't accustomed to feeling such profound gratitude and goodness of the spirit. There were so many negative feelings associated with the Church that had been getting in the way. But thanks to God, my heart only had room for the spirit that evening.

The peace I felt during President Kimball's visit was more profound than the counterfeit peace I had felt while drinking. Through the painful existence of my teenage world came the gracious, gentle reminder that God loves me and that I truly can find peace His Way. He sent me the message with one of his prophets.

I received a deep and undeniable witness that a true prophet of God was sitting on the stand right before me. The diminutive President Kimball stood as living, breathing, gently-speaking proof that God lives, that Jesus is the Christ, and that a modern-day prophet was at the helm.

As far as I knew, a prophet had never visited Las Vegas before – Sin City, the gambling capital of the world. But President Kimball's presence served as the proof I needed to go on and to keep believing. It was as if he were there just for me, proving Heavenly Father and the Savior knew my name and loved me no matter what.

The Lord really could find a lost coin, even if it was lost in Las Vegas.

The eternal plan.

As with the visit from President Kimball, there were other events that continued to nurture my testimony amid the conflict. One such event took place when I went to Lake Mead with a few of my high school friends.

We went to a beach frequented by tourists. Suddenly, a woman started jumping up and down and screaming in a foreign language – Chinese, I think. At first, I thought she was mad at one of her kids but she was yelling hysterically. Finally, she pointed out across the water. I looked over just in time to see some splashing and the tip of a dark head of hair going under.

Without any conscious thought, I dived in and swam to the place where I'd seen the person go under. The water was murky, and it went down about 12 feet. I started diving down to where I thought her child might be, and then I'd come back up for air. A man soon joined me in the search.

After several exhausting dives, I finally came across a human body on the floor of the lake. It was not the body of a child, though. It was a large adult male. I signaled the other searcher, and he swam over to help. I took hold of one side of the body, by the shoulder and chest, while he took the other side. When we pulled the body to the surface, the victim's head bobbed up and out of the water. His eyes were wide open with a frozen look of terror and a vacant look, devoid of his spirit. His skin was an eerie shade of bluish green.

He wasn't responding, or breathing. I gasped.

By then, others had come out in a boat. They took the body to shore where park rangers had just arrived. CPR and mouth-to-mouth were begun while the woman stood by screaming and crying. The rest of us stood by in silence.

After working on the man for quite some time, they quit and stood up. The woman collapsed on top of him. She let out a blood-curdling scream that could be understood in any language. It sounded like her soul was being ripped apart.

The sound was so hollow and haunting. I remember feeling like this woman was sure that her husband was gone forever and she'd never see him again. Ever.

I wanted to comfort her but realized there was nothing I could do. Since she didn't speak English, there was nothing I could say, either. Not that I would have known what to say. But I wished there had been a way, the right time and place, somehow, for me to talk to her about the plan of salvation and temple sealings for time and all eternity.

I felt such a strong conviction of the eternal plan and its importance. How it might bring comfort to the woman now and in the days and weeks to come. Not to mention eternity.

Then I felt a strong impression of the importance of an eternal marriage and an assurance that it was in my future. The impression seemed so real, even though my parents had been married in the temple and were divorced. Even though my same-sex attractions had become stronger. Even though I wasn't sure I could keep going to church much longer.

There, standing on the beach with that woman screaming a hollow scream of inconsolable despair, I heard a still small voice reminding me of Truth, of how I loved it, and of how I could live it.

I had no idea then just how important that impression would prove to be.

MIGHTY CHANGE II

U pon graduation from high school, I attended college with a half-academic, half-athletic scholarship as a microbiology/pre-med major playing softball. Having come from a medical family, I thought becoming a doctor seemed like the logical choice. Unfortunately, my high school study habits – or the lack thereof – came along with me. Worse yet, I discovered I could skip class and nobody seemed to notice or care. I knew I needed good grades to get into medical school, so I did make some effort, most of which consisted of cramming all night before my exams. It didn't help that I had trouble concentrating and finding enough motivation to get through the day. I was battling anxiety and depression, although it would be several years before I learned that.

During spring quarter my freshman year, which was softball season, I had a microbiology class that was only offered in the afternoon and only during spring quarter. That meant I would miss a lot of classes because of softball games. When I told the professor about it, he insisted, "Oh, you can't miss that many lectures and hope to pass. This is a very rigorous course."

I told him I had no choice.

"Well then, you realize if you try and fail, you'll get an F. Don't come crying to me if you can't keep up." He was being funny, but he meant it.

"Okay, as long as you don't come crying to me because someone missed half your lectures and still got an A."

We both laughed.

I'd love to say I was motivated by my desire to succeed. I still hadn't given college my best effort. But this seemed to be a worthy challenge – the chance to prove I was right and the seasoned microbiology professor was wrong. That was true motivation for me. Pathetic, but true.

I worked harder and studied more for that class than any other college course. My stubbornness prevailed. I received an A in the class.

The professor called me into his office. Shaking his head he said, "You got one of the highest grades in the class and you were only there half the time. I've got to admit, you proved me wrong. So, would you like to work in our lab on campus this summer? I could use another teaching assistant for the micro lab next year, too. Are you interested?"

I tried to explain to him that I wasn't really that smart, mostly just stubborn. I'd simply worked hard to prove him wrong. He refused to listen.

So, I worked in his lab and then as a T.A. the following year. That led to a job at a research facility working with embryonic plants. I mostly did grunt work – preparing Petri dishes and dividing cultures. We worked with various types of embryonic plants including jojoba, cactus, and sequoia. The plants were treated with certain hormones in order to keep them from developing normally. They bore very little resemblance to their full-grown counterparts, even though they contained the same genetic material.

Several embryonic plants could be grown in one small Petri dish ¾" tall and 3½" in diameter. Thousands of these Petri dishes fit into one small culture room. Because of this, experiments could be performed that normally required hundreds of acres if full-grown plants were used.

The process of growing plants in their embryonic form can also be reversed. They become fully-developed plants when they're treated with the proper compounds because they contain the same genetic material.

I found the embryonic sequoias to be most interesting. Those amazing miniature sprigs were grown to about an inch or so in height or length. Then, at that point, we'd divide them using a tiny scalpel like miniature pruning shears. Eight sequoias fit into a Petri dish.

In contrast, full-sized giant sequoias grow to more than 250 feet tall. The largest is the General Sherman tree, which is 32 feet in diameter. The other variety of sequoia, the redwood, grows to more than 300 feet tall. I've stood right next to one–which is the finest way to experience a sequoia–and I've followed all 300-plus feet up to where it pokes a hole in the azure blue field of sky. It evokes such an awesome sense of the power and glory of creation.

Never in a million years would you guess that, treated with the right compounds, those tiny eight-to-a-Petri-dish sprigs could become magnificent 300-foot sequoias. Treat them correctly and they'll reach their full potential.

Life is like that. God knows our full potential, and how

we can achieve it–here on earth as well as in the next life. He sees and acknowledges the works that we have already accomplished. He is fully aware of our divine heritage and the fact that our eternal self has ultimate power over our human imperfections and the natural man.

At that time in my life, I guess you could say I was unable to see over the side of the Petri dish. I couldn't really see or comprehend my divine heritage. Little did I know that the potential was there, not in spite of my earthly challenges, rather, in part, because of them.

The trials I was facing did not disprove my divine nature. They were preparing me for it. Refining me and calling for sacrifices I did not yet know how to make.

The grandeur and magnificence of our divine nature, our potential to become gods someday, can be difficult to imagine or comprehend while we're here on earth, struggling to see beyond the Petri dish.

My wide world of sports.

College softball was my one reprieve. Because practice began in the fall, I was able to make friends right when I started college. Practices were rigorous and challenging, yet fun. Playing sports served as an escape just like it had in high school. I seldom if ever missed practice, and dedicated myself to softball. By the start of my freshman season, I'd earned myself a spot on the starting line-up.

I attended church at a student ward in the beginning. Unfortunately, I felt worse about myself every time I went. The things forbidden by the Church had the greatest allure. My attraction toward women increased. I started partying with other athletes on occasion, using alcohol or marijuana to relax and escape.

Eventually, I quit going to church altogether. I was tired of all the guilt, self-hatred and conflict. There also seemed to be better things to do on Sundays than go to church. My testimony remained even though I whittled away at it with rationalizations, telling myself I would return to the Church someday when it wasn't so hard to go.

Hah! I had no idea how much harder it would be to make the return trip.

About two-thirds of the women on my college softball team were attracted to other women, as near as I could tell. It wasn't easy to know for sure. Most people weren't talking very openly about being gay or lesbian in the late 70s.

My sophomore year, I concentrated on softball and little else. I had the highest batting average in the league going into the last few games of the season. Then, during a key double-header, I tore my anterior cruciate ligament off the bone. The surgery was on my 20th birthday. The doctor and nurses sang "Happy Birthday" as I was going under. They performed a now-antiquated procedure in which they made a 7-inch incision on one side of my leg and a 3-inch incision on the other side, and then stapled the ligament back onto the bone.

I was barely able to attend the regional tournament. I had to drag myself to the stands using crutches, trying to maneuver a very sore leg that had a cast from my ankle to my hip. I sat there, helpless, while I watched my nationally-ranked team lose. It was gut-wrenching.

When they announced the All-Conference players there

at regionals, I was thrilled to be among them. However, it was bittersweet. I had to hobble down from the stands and accept my award, standing there on crutches while all the other women were in uniform.

That knee injury was a crushing blow. It brought my healthiest coping mechanism to an abrupt halt. Softball, the one thing I loved, the sport for which my dad taught me to "throw like a girl with a really good arm," the thing I really excelled at, was taken right out from under me.

I was in a cast for three months. After a month into it, I started going stir crazy. I could no longer use sports as an escape or use the endorphins from rigorous physical activity to ward off my depression and anxiety. I started drinking and smoking pot and tobacco on a regular basis, rather than just occasionally. By the time my cast was taken off, there was so much atrophy in my leg and instability in my knee that it never fully recovered, despite the two-hour-a-day therapy that was soon added to my regular softball workout.

Relationships with women.

No doubt my complete abandonment of the Word of Wisdom made it that much easier for me to break other commandments. I soon became involved with a girlfriend of mine. It never got too physical because of my testimony. I knew it wasn't right, from a gospel perspective. However, from a personal and emotional perspective, it certainly felt right. So many feelings I'd kept buried came to the surface.

It felt natural to me. I was not the least bit repulsed by it, although I'd wondered if I might be. Culture and religion taught me well that you don't get involved with members of the same sex: it's revolting, foul, and disgusting. I found it to be the opposite.

I appreciated the fact that the relationship was casual. It gave me the time to explore my feelings. I quickly learned that yes, indeed, I did like women.

Regardless of who disapproved, there was a matter that must be reckoned with. I didn't say the word "gay" or "lesbian" with regard to myself at that time. Still, my feelings were out. I was out.

Questions turned to answers. Hesitation turned to exhilaration. I was finally free!

Or was I?

When school started again in the fall, I became quite busy with classes, softball practice and physical therapy. I played softball with good women and formed close friendships that I still cherish to this day. Road trips made for some great times on and off the field. We had a lot of fun and it helped make life much more enjoyable. Often there was a party or get-together at somebody's place–usually mine. We'd play cards or watch a movie or get drunk, or all of the above. Since many of them were lesbian, we'd go to gay bars on occasion. We also enjoyed hiking and camping whenever we got the chance.

My performance during the softball season my junior year was a huge disappointment. Despite the hundreds of hours I'd committed above and beyond, I couldn't perform as well as I did the previous year. The strength difference between my two legs was an issue. The knee itself was a problem, too. It frequently hurt, and in order to play, I had to wear a very large, cumbersome metal brace. The mental aspects of the injury also affected me. And I was partying quite often. That surely didn't help.

Rather than serving as an escape for me, softball became a source of stress and frustration. After the season was over, I decided it wouldn't be worth my time, or anyone else's, if I were to play my senior year. I also decided I didn't want to go into medicine, so I wasn't even sure I wanted to finish my microbiology degree.

Everything was so up in the air. My life became filled with uncertainty. What would I major in now? Where would I go to school? What would I do for a living?

When my future was totally in question, I met Tracy. She quickly became my entire answer.

I was thrilled, but also scared. Up until that point, I was mostly curious about my attraction to women, without putting too much permanence to it. I determined it might just be a phase. I still held to the idea that at some point, I could simply return to the gospel, if I were so inclined.

But then I fell in love. And I was in love with a woman.

I hadn't actually planned to fall in love with a woman. I'd forgotten the fact that you don't really plan such things. If you're attracted to women and you date them, well, there's a pretty good chance you'll fall in love with one.

I'd never experienced such excitement and joy and all the other sensations that come with infatuation and falling in love. It was fantasy turned reality. I finally found relief from the pain without abusing drugs and alcohol, which Tracy discouraged. I began to feel love and acceptance because of who I was, not because of what I did or did not do. I finally felt safe, understood, accepted and loved.

Tracy and I were a lot alike. We related in many of the same ways. At church, I had felt rejection. With Tracy, I felt acceptance. Finally, something felt right and good in my life.

At least, it felt right and good until a problem arose: my testimony of the gospel of Jesus Christ. I'd try to block it out with Tracy, or drugs and alcohol when she wasn't around, but it kept nagging at me. I could not become completely comfortable with the physical aspects of our relationship because of my testimony. And I was never very honest with Tracy about it. I kept trying to hide the conflict that was, no doubt, quite evident.

We lived together for a time. However, conflicts kept arising. Eventually Tracy left, in search of a more stable relationship. I became angry at God for supposedly causing me to be so unsteady in the relationship. I was heartbroken and blamed Him for it.

It seemed like such a cruel joke! How could God allow any of His children to be attracted to the same sex as their only expression of love and then expect them not to be involved in such relationships?

It didn't seem fair. It didn't seem loving. It didn't seem right. And the turmoil it created seemed unbearable.

A woman's search for happiness.

I had some sort of moral breakdown after Tracy. The deep despair over losing her was combined with my anger toward, and doubts concerning, God. The relationship with Tracy had felt so right, as long as I wasn't feeling conflicted by my testimony.

Because I felt miserable without Tracy, I erroneously

concluded that the gospel must be wrong and my relationship with Tracy had been right. I made a conscious decision to abandon my testimony and all of its ridiculous rules.

Tragically, I had no idea where the ridiculous rules ended and my own personal values began. I threw out the baby with the baptism water. I decided there were no rules with regard to the Word of Wisdom or that bothersome law of chastity that had wreaked havoc in my life.

I partied and tried whatever drugs came my way. I dated different women and tried to make myself interested even when I wasn't. I kept trying to fill the huge void I felt without Tracy. I desperately wanted relief.

I went out of town one weekend with some friends. We checked into a hotel and I went to the bar for drinks. A guy came over and sat down next to me. He seemed interested in me but was okay with just talking.

As I started getting drunk, I got a brilliant idea—at least it seemed brilliant while I was drunk. I decided I could prove I was "normal," a "heterosexual" like most people, by having sex with this man.

So, I invited him up to my room. I'm sure he expected to have sex. I thought we would, too. By the time we got up to my room and started kissing, I changed my mind. I just couldn't go through with it. I didn't want to have sex with some stranger, especially not a man. I didn't even want to be kissing him.

I pushed away as he held on. I pushed some more, and he backed off. Not really knowing what to do, I saw the mini bar and suggested we have more to drink. I was already fairly inebriated and unable to determine that I was making the situation worse. I became really nervous and surprisingly afraid to be assertive. (Later I learned I was freezing up, as if I were a victim again, feeling unable to stop a man.)

I don't remember how many mini bottles I downed before I said I was tired and laid down on the bed to sleep. When I awoke, he was on top of me. I didn't have much strength or capacity to resist as he forced himself on me.

When he was finished, he got dressed and headed for the door. I stared at him, trying to process what had just happened. All he said was, "You know why you asked me up here. We both got what we wanted."

It certainly wasn't what I wanted. I wanted to feel normal, whatever that meant. I wanted to get rid of the self-hatred, shame and isolation. Instead, it just intensified.

The next morning, I felt so dirty. I took a long shower, desperately scrubbing myself in an attempt to wash off the filth, to wash that man off of me. Try as I might, no amount of scouring could help me feel clean. To add to the pain of it all, I had to worry about whether or not I'd gotten pregnant or contracted a sexually-transmitted disease.

I took all the blame for yet another forced sexual encounter. After all, I was the one who invited the guy up to my room. I just couldn't believe I'd done something so stupid. The only thing I'd proven was that I was a wreck.

I remember looking into the mirror and feeling like I didn't know who was staring back at me. I was doing things I'd never done before and never thought I'd be doing.

I continued to date women in an effort to find what I hoped would be a healthy relationship. Eventually I met Kathy. She and I became involved for several months before

I decided to move out of state and go to art school. I wanted something different and hoped I might be able to change other aspects of my life, too.

After I moved, Kathy flew out to see me several times. Her visits helped with the loneliness. But, in between visits, I had a chance to ponder. Christ took those moments, as fleeting as they were, to reach out to me. Deep down inside, I still had a testimony of The Church of Jesus Christ of Latter-day Saints. Regardless of what I did, it would not go away.

In a desperate search for relief, I did some calling around and found the phone number of the man who was the bishop of the singles ward I apparently lived in. I called him and we set up a meeting for the following Sunday.

I was so nervous about telling a complete stranger the most intimate details of my life, especially a man. Worse yet, I had to tell him I'd been sexually involved with women.

I managed to show up and meet with the bishop because I knew it was the right thing to do. By the grace of God, that man was one of the finest Christians I have ever met. Bishop Garey was filled with the Spirit and spoke in such a way that his words resonated truth as well as understanding, compassion and empathy.

After our first meeting, Bishop Garey asked if we could meet every week. I looked forward to those meetings and quickly came to depend on them. Although I had difficulty feeling the spirit on my own or at church, I always felt it when we met. He was supportive and asked me to break off ties with Kathy. I told him I'd work on it.

I was helped with the breakup after I experienced one of the most humiliating events of my life. Kathy came out to see me and got a ride with Peggy, a mutual friend of ours. Peggy's sister and her family lived about 20 miles from me, so I picked Kathy up from there. After the weekend was over, I drove her back.

It was Sunday and Peggy's sister, who was an active Mormon, left for church with her husband and kids. The three of us sat around and talked for a bit. Then Kathy and I went into one of the bedrooms to say goodbye. I laid down on the bed and then Kathy laid down on top of me.

Suddenly, the bedroom door opened, followed by a shriek. We looked over to see Peggy's sister standing there. She quickly backed out and slammed the door.

My heart sank. Kathy and I just stared at each other, not knowing what to say or do. It was an awful feeling.

Then Peggy came into the room. "My sister's really upset. Let's just go."

Apparently, Peggy's sister had come home from church early because her little boy was sick. We were in his bedroom, and she was coming in to get his pajamas.

Kathy and I left the house and went to our separate cars. Just as I was getting into my car, Peggy came out with her sister, who was crying. I got back out of the car and walked toward them. I really wanted to apologize.

Peggy's sister got this horrified, disgusted, furious look on her face. It was an expression I hope I never see again.

Holding out her hands, palms forward like a traffic cop, she yelled, "Don't come near me!"

I stopped in my tracks. From halfway across the lawn I said, "I just want to say I'm sorry."

"How could you, in MY house? What if my little boy had

been the one to walk in on you?"

A deep pang shot straight through me. Then, years of shame began to well up in my heart and spill over as tears.

"I'm just so sorry," I uttered as I turned around and got back in my car.

I didn't drive very far before I had to pull over. Collapsing over the steering wheel, I began to sob. Not just because of what had happened at the house, in case that weren't bad enough. But also because of all the guilt and shame that had been piling up in my subconscious and conscious that came crashing down. Shame for "breaking the law of chastity" when I was 10, and again so many times. Shame for having attractions to women, as if that were somehow my fault. Shame for being such a "sick" person, as if that were true. And, shame for taking something unwanted into the home of a Latter-day Saint family, which was, indeed, my fault.

Was I really so disgusting that someone couldn't stand the very sight of me?

Was I really such a pervert?

Was there any hope for me?

No.

There was no hope.

No reason for living.

Plenty of reasons for dying.

Being me became more than I could bear. I started the car again and drove down the freeway. The despair, the loneliness and the futility were laid bare. As I came to a large cement pylon below an overpass, I decided to drive head on into it. But when I went to turn the wheel towards it, I just couldn't do it. As I continued driving, each overpass represented an opportunity to end it all. To finally do away with the person who seemed to be making the world a far worse place to live, especially my own world.

Although I never would have considered myself worthy at the time, looking back, I'm certain there were angels helping to keep my car on course. Helping to keep me alive.

After I got home, I drank and drank and drank some more in an effort to drown out the voices of despair. I wanted to slow my thoughts, to get them stumbling about in a drunken stupor rather than racing through my head with hazardous messages of self-loathing and hopelessness.

Still, the thoughts remained. What kind of Latter-day Saint woman is attracted to other women? Really, how could I be such a mess? Lesbian and Latter-day Saint! Alcoholic! Sinner! Truly, there is no hope.

At some point, I guess I passed out.

A sense of belonging, or lack thereof.

I managed to hang on by a thread until the next meeting with my bishop. I told him what had happened and then I expressed my shame. He was so encouraging and kind. He reminded me that I was a beloved daughter of God, and that he loved me, too. He said how I was of worth, regardless of my struggles. He expressed his faith in my ability to work through my attractions to women and my dependence on drugs and alcohol, with the Lord's help. He promised he'd be with me every step of the way, too. He encouraged regular scripture study, prayer and church attendance.

I believed him. I always felt that I could believe him.

So, I began attending church every week. I didn't know

anyone there and felt so out of place. I was the misfit, the pervert, the queer. The vile, repulsive sinner. There I'd sit in the back of the chapel, fidgeting around on the bench, hoping no one suspected who I really was.

There's nothing lonelier than sitting in a room full of people who don't understand.

I went to Relief Society one Sunday. As the sisters filtered in, they talked and laughed with one another. I sat back and watched from behind what felt like a partition. I was the outsider looking in, observing life in Relief Society as if it were a moving diorama at a visitors' center.

I longed for my old friends and my previous way of life. Those people understood me and accepted me for who I was, whoever that might be. They seemed to know, better than anyone else in the world, how I felt. They didn't cringe at the sight of me, or condemn me. They never rejected or shamed me. They'd already experienced enough of that in their own lives.

Gay bashing–physically and verbally–was very popular and more widely accepted back then. I just assumed I knew how the ward members would react if they knew about me. At church and church-related events, I'd hear some unchristian comments about gays, followed by loud laughter.

The Mormon Church. Would I ever belong?

Shelter from the storm.

I began drinking and using drugs quite heavily as I tried to endure the indescribable pain. I felt completely shut off from human contact and love. The bishop was a wonderful man, but he could only do so much. I felt no connection with anyone in the ward and so much connection with my other group of friends.

During the next six months, I did make some progress. I broke up with Kathy. I kept myself cut off from those who added to my longing for lesbian relationships.

Then I made the mistake of visiting Tracy, just to say goodbye for good. When we got together, we discovered our feelings for each other were stronger than ever. We decided to start seeing each other again.

I was elated. It was such a rush. I felt so alive, especially after spending months wishing I were dead.

It felt so right with Tracy, better than ever before. I figured I just needed to get rid of my testimony of the gospel and the Church's prejudiced policies, and then Tracy and I could be happy together.

I went to see Bishop Garey, to tell him that I wouldn't be coming back to church. I really did like him and I knew he cared about me, for which I was grateful. I told him that I appreciated his help but I'd decided to live with Tracy again, in a lesbian relationship "where I belonged." I told him he could go ahead and take my name off the Church records. I thought once my name was removed, I wouldn't have to worry about the LDS Church anymore.

I breathed a sigh of relief and got up to leave. Bishop Garey asked if he could say something before I left. Of course he could. I'd come to trust and respect the man.

As he began to speak, an intensity of spirit entered the room that pierced my heart and soul. He warned me that if I walked away from the Church, I'd never return and my life would turn to hell.

I was immediately struck down by his words, unable to speak or move. I sat there, motionless in the chair.

For a moment—for what seemed like an eternity—the spirit of Christ was taken away from me. I felt what true darkness and isolation were like, which was worse than what I'd been feeling the past few months.

I discovered that the Spirit I thought had flickered out was still a vital life force I desperately needed. And wanted.

If those had simply been the words of a bishop, I would have stormed out of his office and never looked back. However, I knew I'd received a hand-delivered message from beyond the veil. I knew the message was Truth.

I'd already learned that whenever I turned my back on the Church and the Lord, my life careened out of control.

What was I thinking?

What was I feeling?

What could I do?

The darkness that fell after Bishop Garey spoke was slightly lifted when a faint glimmer of hope flickered. I sensed that Christ Himself was calling me back, begging me to come unto Him and receive His Light. Letting me know that it was truly possible.

The bishop reassured me, too. He bore a strong witness that the Lord had a special purpose in store for me and that was why the adversary was working so hard to discourage and distract me.

He read the scripture: "For whom the Lord loveth he chasteneth".[1] He said that chasten meant to discipline and, more importantly, it also meant to purify and refine. He then continued reading in Hebrews 12.

"Now no chastening for the present seemeth to be joyous, but grievous: nevertheless afterward it yieldeth the peaceable fruit of righteousness unto them which are exercised thereby. Wherefore lift up the hands which hang down, and the feeble knees; And make straight paths for your feet, lest that which is lame be turned out of the way; but let it rather be healed."[2]

I wanted to be healed.

I can still feel the power and impact of that meeting with the bishop. It has been called to my remembrance many times over the years. It has served as a tangible reminder of right and wrong, truth and error, darkness and light. And that I greatly prefer the Light.

Pain's stranglehold.

Even though I had a renewed resolve from my meeting with the bishop and I had felt the light of Christ, there was still Tracy. She was tough competition for a flicker of light.

I could feel her love. She was right there for me. When I prayed for comfort from heaven, I often could not feel it.

Tracy was tangible. The Spirit of Christ was not.

The battle that ensued was horrendous. There was a constant struggle between what felt right and what I knew to be right. I'd had a firm knowledge and testimony of the gospel of Jesus Christ for as long as I could remember. But my testimony seemed to be working against me now. It had gone beyond feeling and existed as a cold, hard fact.

I'd never doubted the gospel of Jesus Christ before. Now I had to. It lacked the *feeling* of rightness I had with Tracy. It was telling me that what felt right was actually wrong.

I continued to pray, even though I couldn't feel the spirit. I had the faith that it might make a difference somehow.

Bishop Garey asked me if I could cut off my relationship with Tracy and I told him I couldn't. My feelings were far too strong, and I felt little comfort at church. So he asked me not to see her for as long as I could.

When I felt I couldn't handle being away from her any longer, I told the bishop I had to see her. I assured him nothing would happen, honestly believing it wouldn't. But when something did happen, I sheepishly returned to the bishop looking for his help and guidance, and forgiveness.

My life became a cycle of stepping out into the storm, feeling unable to survive the loneliness and the bitter cold, and returning to the only warmth and shelter that I knew.

"But when he saw the wind boisterous, he was afraid; and beginning to sink, he cried, saying, Lord, save me."[3] I just kept sinking.

As the cycle repeated itself, I abused drugs and alcohol in an attempt to fix the pain. The darkness was all-consuming. It felt like my very identity was being ripped apart. I suppose that's exactly what was happening.

I kept praying and reading scriptures and attending church on occasion. But when I needed strength from the Lord, I often could not grasp it. Looking back, I'm sure He was holding out His hand, but I felt unworthy to respond. I mistakenly believed His love had to be earned.

The heavens seemed like brass. The conflict was intolerable. What felt right was wrong. What felt wrong was right. Nothing made any sense, and nobody had any real answers. No one could make it better.

When the pain became more excruciating than I could bear, I took the gun I used for protection from beneath my bed, pulled back the hammer, and put the gun to my head.

Try as I might, I could not pull the trigger.

It was neither cowardice nor bravery that stopped me. It was the impression that a bullet would not end my turmoil. I needed to fight the battle on this frontier.

I put the gun away, but got it back out again and again whenever life became unbearable.

The one person who could bring the Truth and Light of the gospel to the dark abyss was Bishop Garey. Whenever I'd tell him about the horrible pain, he empathized with my struggle. He showed incredible compassion and understanding. His empathy gave me the impression that he was no stranger to depression. I felt he had walked a path similar to mine, through the valley of the shadow of death.

Later, I would discover just how well he understood.

There were times I would lie in bed, unable to sit up, even when I wrote in my journal. I was no longer worried about who might read it. Many pages consisted of chicken scribbles slanting down the page.

Pain seldom stays within the lines.

There were many dark and empty days where I questioned whether I could make it. I felt like I was fighting the inevitable. "I'm gay," I'd cry, in an attempt to get God to face the facts. One day I wrote:

> Dear God, it's black again.
> Two solid months of darkness.
> Two solid days of light marked Christ's arrival.

I guess He isn't coming.

Have faith, you say?
But faith does not hold my hand.
Or stroke my hair
And tell me I'm OK.

God, if this is wrong,
Then where's thy love when heaven's touch
Feels cold as brass?

And if this flame that lights my heart
Is Satan's fire, I cannot tell.
Sheep's clothing warms my soul.

You say to change.
I say I can't.
I feel, therefore I am.

"Wherever two or more are gathered."

Sometimes I'd sit in this tiny sunroom with a solitary chair that had my scriptures next to it. That's where I'd go to read in hopes of surviving another day. Somehow, some way, the scriptures helped – like an I.V. drip providing just enough nutrients to keep me alive.

Drip.

Drip.

Drip.

I wanted to "feast upon the words of Christ,"[4] but I was not accustomed to finding nourishment the Lord's way. And so it came, drip by drip, line upon line, here a little, there a little. It never seemed to be enough. I was in constant pain. But I kept going back to the scriptures for more nourishment because I was acting on faith.

Bishop Garey continued to be a mighty source of strength and Light. He was like a second father to me. I loved my dad, but he'd been completely inactive in the Church since the divorce. It was nice to have someone who held the priesthood and who held the mantle in my behalf.

I always signed up for the first weekly appointment with the bishop. I'd sit on the front steps of the chapel every Wednesday night waiting for him to arrive. He'd drive up, then walk over and put his arm around me and ask how I was doing. After unlocking the door to the church, he would escort me in. It was always dark, until he'd turn on the light. I remember thinking how symbolic that was. My life was dark except for when the bishop turned on the Light.

After asking how I was doing, he'd smile and say something encouraging. Even when I'd fallen, he would offer support. I basked in the Spirit that emanated from him. He always read a scripture that applied to my situation. When there were certain things I was not yet strong enough to stop doing, he'd give me weekly assignments that I *could* do. Those things would strengthen my self-confidence and my spirituality. It was obvious how much he genuinely cared about me. His love strengthened my motivation to keep trying to do what was right.

I loved those twenty minutes with him and hated to have them end.

My prayers started to break through the cloud cover on

occasion. I'd kneel in prayer–many times a day–begging for strength. Heavenly Father was the one person with whom I could be completely open and honest. My anger toward Him started to diminish as I befriended Him and felt His continual attempts to embrace me.

I finally found the nerve to confide in a friend from the ward. Leeza started out as my visiting teacher, assigned by the bishop and the Relief Society president. Initially she was told that I needed some special attention. We soon became good friends and, with the bishop's encouragement, I told her that I struggled with homosexual desires and substance abuse. She was supportive and discreet, and her reaction encouraged me to tell another friend. It was such a welcome relief to spend time with two Mormon women who knew all about me, accepted me, and loved me regardless.

When Leeza was called as Relief Society president, she kept herself on as my visiting teacher and also helped me get to know more people in the ward. I began to feel a sense of belonging in a church that once felt so rejecting.

Finding people who were Christlike in their reactions helped me better understand how the gospel was designed to work. I learned not to lump everything and everyone into "the Church." Yes, some people at church, including a few leaders, misunderstood the challenges for Latter-day Saints with same-sex attraction. Sometimes they were harsh in their judgments and made insensitive comments. However, I met others at church who were very supportive and nonjudgmental. That made such a difference for me.

Most importantly, I knew that Christ understands, and He is at the head of the Church.

Exposing a counterfeit.

My increased involvement at church and friendships with ward members helped me gain the strength to stop seeing Tracy, for good. Unfortunately, I still felt a void and kept pouring alcohol into it. I used drugs sometimes, too, and it was a blessing I didn't become addicted to cocaine. That held the greatest threat, not only because of the physical dangers, but also because it helped me feel good about myself, even though it was a counterfeit confidence. With it, I felt like I could succeed and accomplish anything, which contrasted with my typical feelings of failure and shame.

One evening, I was using cocaine with Brent, a friend of mine. After using all his cocaine by 2:30 in the morning, I wasn't ready to stop. So, when he offered to take me to his supplier's house, I agreed.

We took a cab to the heart of a notorious drug neighborhood. I was somewhat nervous, but my need to get high was greater than my fear. Brent told the cabby to pull over. The driver said, "Miss, are you sure you want to get out here? This is a dangerous neighborhood." Oh yes, I wanted to get out there, thank you.

We went in and Brent asked for rock cocaine – the form in which it's smoked. Nearly all the house lights were out to avoid suspicion because the area was frequently patrolled. The woman's grandfather sat in a rocker, peeking through a slit in the curtains, watching for cops.

The three of us smoked everything Brent bought, which lasted till sunup. Then the woman's young son walked into the room. I was aghast that he came in while we had been using drugs.

{ 73 }

Without skipping a beat, the young boy asked, "Do you want me to make another run?"

"Yeah, hurry." Brent handed him a fistful of bills, and the boy skipped off as if he were going to the neighbor's house to borrow a couple of eggs or something. He was eight or nine, around baptismal age.

I watched that kid run out the door, then looked at that grandpa peering out the window as a ray of sunlight from heaven came shining through the curtains and I felt the strongest desire to be home. I'm not sure whose home. I just wanted to be in a good Mormon home where the kids went off to Primary to learn about the Savior and grandpa sat in an easy chair reading the scriptures.

That experience cured me of my cocaine abuse, although I continued to drink. I also kept praying and going to church and meeting with the bishop. As I continued to put forth consistent effort, good days increased and my substance abuse subsided.

In addition, I'd stopped visiting Tracy, stopped going anywhere I was more likely to meet women seeking homosexual relationships, and consistently avoided thinking of other women in ways I shouldn't.

It was like being on a roller coaster. I'd work hard and be doing well, and then I would fall straight down again. It felt like I was right back where I started from, but I wasn't. I just didn't realize I had been learning and growing. I was being strengthened as I exercised my faith again and again. And my unwanted desires were becoming less intense.

I'd go up and down, then a little further up and not quite as far down. On and on it went as I moved forward in faith.

Tender mercy #2,134.

Many times when I felt like I wasn't going to make it, the Lord would step in with a tender mercy. I explained one such incident in my journal:

"For the past few weeks I've been slipping back into that bottomless pit. I could feel the adversary's hot breath and hear that horrid gnashing of teeth. Yesterday I felt overwhelmed. I decided failure was just a matter of time and I couldn't handle failing again.

"I had to work far into the night, and I was exhausted. I felt completely hopeless, so I decided to pray. I was tired of asking for strength. I was tired of 'having faith.' I was tired of 'trusting God.' I was tired.

"Somehow, I mustered up a 'Heavenly Father, I need help or I'm not going to make it. I can't do this anymore. Amen.' I didn't think much about it, only that I felt really disappointed I couldn't utter some profound prayer that would bring down the powers of heaven. I needed that so desperately.

"I finished my work and went outside for some air. The whole world was asleep. There were clouds blowing across the sky, much closer than usual. And every chance the moon got, it would come blaring through.

"Suddenly, the veil was lifted for a fraction of a second, if eternities can be measured in seconds, and I saw the moon as a heavenly creation. It represented a world like the one I could help create someday–with a husband, no less. I felt I could reach up and grab the moon and start molding it. I have never had the 'life beyond' seem so real, and so attainable. It was like Heavenly Father was saying, 'You really can do this someday. You will do this someday.'

"It only lasted for an instant. I kept staring at the moon, hoping it would happen again. But mortality returned as quickly as it left. This morning I burned the toast, spent an hour looking for my keys, and got a phone call from Tracy. So much for godhood."

That impression reminded me of another one I'd had years before: the experience on the beach when the woman lost her husband and I felt impressed that a temple marriage was in my future. I'd received two witnesses that an eternal marriage was within my grasp.

After that, I did not fall again with regard to homosexual transgression. I had my doubts and was tempted, but I never succumbed. I think part of me knew I really couldn't handle that again. Heavenly Father must have known, too, because He stepped in so majestically and with such mercy.

I'd never really thought of Heavenly Father as being merciful until then. I thought He was cold and demanding. I didn't trust Him. I didn't think He answered my prayers.

But perhaps God really did answer prayers. Maybe He was willing to help. Maybe He didn't consider me to be some pervert unworthy of His attention.

Gradually, the spiritual feelings became more frequent and they started to linger. They began to "enlighten my understanding" and "to be delicious to me."[5] They brought more peace and satisfaction, so I started desiring them more than homosexual relationships. The changes weren't all that noticeable at the time. But in hindsight, it's obvious that they were part of a divine pattern.

I finally graduated from college–having changed my major and gone to college for another four years. It wasn't easy finding a local job in advertising. So, while I was looking, the bishop offered to let me work at his office. I got to see him in a different environment. He was almost as great a businessman as he was spiritual leader. It also helped to have the bishop around all day, making it much easier to do the right things. I'm sure Bishop Garey thought of that.

After exhausting all of the local job possibilities, I began to look out of state. Of course, just my luck, I found a job in no time. I didn't really want to move because I'd been doing well and had so much support in the ward. However, Bishop Garey felt inspired that I should take the job. In opposition to what I wanted to do, I felt like he was right.

Before I left, Bishop Garey gave me a blessing. It was so powerful, even prophetic. He spoke of things the Lord had in store for me. It felt like a father's blessing, some of the things a father would say if a child were moving away from home. In fact, near the end of the blessing he said something I've always cherished: "I love you as if you were a fruit of my loins." I felt the same way. I loved him as a second father.

Apparently, it was time for me to move on. I packed up my belongings and moved to a new state. I was determined to start a new life, with Bishop Garey's support via phone.

Two months after the move, I wrote in my journal:

"I have lost so much time. Can I ever regain it? Will I ever become the person the Lord and I want me to be? It seems like I have so far to go. But perhaps it always seems that way. Once again, the key word is patience. I'm just so sick and tired of being patient."

Burying faith.

It took me awhile to adjust to a new city and settle into a new routine. I remained determined to be obedient to the Word of Wisdom, sometimes slipping up but never giving up. Over a period of several months, I managed to turn completely to the Lord and stop using altogether.

I considered calling Bishop Garey to tell him. He'd been released as bishop, and we'd been talking less often since I'd made friends in my new ward. I knew he'd be pleased, but decided to wait and call him after I'd been sober even longer.

Then Leeza called, saying she had terrible news. Bishop Garey had died unexpectedly. I asked her how it had happened. She just started talking about the funeral. I asked her again. That's when she told me our beloved bishop shot himself in the head.

I was unable to respond.

Or think.

Or put one word where it belonged . . . after another word?

or before

should it be before?

Why?

Why me?

Why the bishop?

How could God possibly think I could handle this?

I'd done my best to be obedient. I'd opened up to my bishop like I was supposed to. He was the reason I made it back into the fold. He was the one who loved me when I was struggling so desperately. He was the one who helped me when I put a gun to *my* head.

Now *he* shot himself in the head?

That couldn't be right!

It didn't make any sense.

That's not how it's supposed to happen.

Apparently, he had bipolar disorder and made the same mistake others have made. Because he'd been feeling better, he assumed that he could quit taking his medication. Then he sunk into a severe depression and had to be hospitalized. The doctors had a difficult time getting it under control. They thought he was ready to go home. They were wrong.

The news was too much for me to bear. I went numb, to the frozen post-trauma place yet again. I remained like that until I flew in for the funeral. Leeza picked me up from the airport and let me stay at her place. Neither one of us really knew what to say. We didn't want to talk about the bishop but everything else seemed too trivial to discuss.

I didn't cry until we got to the church. I walked off by myself and sat on the steps at the side of the church where I could be alone. Very alone. I found myself thinking that if I just sat on the steps long enough, surely the bishop would arrive and come over to give me a nourishing embrace and walk me into the dark chapel and turn on the light for me and reassure me that it was all going to be OK – and I would believe him. I could always believe the bishop.

That's when the dam broke. All the sadness and sorrow and anger I'd kept inside came rushing out. I collapsed in a heap and started sobbing for who knows how long. Finally, the man who used to be the bishop's first counselor came over and helped me up. He gave me a hug and consoled me.

It seemed like since the bishop couldn't be there, he'd sent his first counselor to help me out. It was another tender mercy that the Lord, and perhaps the bishop, had a hand in.

I managed to quit crying and go inside.

Bishop Garey's family had asked members of the singles ward to sing as a choir. I joined them on the stand and sat by Leeza on the front row. I managed to keep it all together until we sang, "God Be With You Till We Meet Again."

Actually, I kept it together until the second verse.

"God be with you till we meet again. When life's perils thick confound you, Put his arms unfailing round you."[6]

I started crying, uncontrollably, there on the front row of the choir on the stand in front of the vast congregation with standing room only. I dropped down in my chair and slumped over. I kept crying as the choir sang on. Leeza put her hand on my shoulder. That made me cry even harder.

After the funeral services, they carried his coffin out of the chapel and turned off my light. Hope disappeared into the bleakness. My faith was buried along with my bishop.

The well of water springing up unto everlasting life.

The battle became horrendous yet again. Why should I

keep trying it God's way? I hadn't seen any mighty changes, only mighty pain. How could any of it be true?

I'd show God He had pushed me too far this time. So, I poured more and more alcohol into the void. Suicide became an option again.

My life careened out of control. I knew I was in trouble, and something had to change or I'd be dead soon. Even though part of me didn't care, another part of me wanted to live. And to do what was right.

How would I be able to put the pieces of my faith back together after they'd been shattered in the fray? What about the safe, comforting truths I'd learned in the innocence of Primary? Back then, everything made sense. Now, nothing made sense. Even when I chose the right there was trauma.

I'd built my house upon the rock but when the rains came down and the floods came up, my life washed away.

That's when Heavenly Father lovingly stepped in again. The same Heavenly Father I had refused to trust. The One I was so angry with, I'd stopped talking to. The One whose Church I'd quit attending.

His Holy Spirit broke through the anger, doubt, and confusion, inspiring me to call a counselor.

Once again, someone was brought into my life just in time to help. Many of the feelings I had for Tracy and other women surfaced again. I seriously doubted I could continue to avoid homosexual relationships or overcome substance abuse. I doubted I could do the "church bit" again.

Miraculously Pam, my counselor, helped to bring hope

back into my life. She had a very strong spirit, and I could feel it. As with Bishop Garey, I gained strength from sitting in a room with someone who was exercising the gifts of the Holy Spirit in my behalf. She was also very gifted as a counselor. She offered practical solutions that helped with my substance abuse and homosexual feelings.

I quit taking a Pollyanna-like view of homosexual relationships and thought of the turmoil that they caused rather than the comfort they provided. I concentrated more on what I truly wanted out of life, and Pam helped me see that I could attain it.

She helped most by bringing the Spirit to our sessions, putting my name on the temple's prayer roll, encouraging me to pray and read scriptures, recommending conference talks and books she thought would help, working with me on my relationships with Christ and Heavenly Father, and helping me understand how to overcome sinful desires.

Emotionally and psychologically, she helped by using therapeutic techniques to help me rethink my thinking, feel differently in response to my thoughts, and understand how I could reshape my desires.

I looked at myself more positively–sexual attractions and all–and my self-hatred and shame began to subside. I attended Alcoholics Anonymous, which emphasized the importance of turning my life over to God and remembering that He knows best for my life. I read scriptures, prayed, and attended church every week.

Gradually, day after day, line upon line, Light entered

my life again. I finally regained sobriety. There were times when every minute of every hour of every day ticked slowly and loudly by. Other times I felt more confident in myself and in heaven's help.

After a year of sobriety, I lapsed again. Fortunately, I got back on track. I became spiritually stronger as my desires to abuse substances became weaker. Desires to be in a lesbian relationship began fading away, too.

A journal entry from that time period reads: "There is a stream of unconsciousness that flows deep within me. It's the love of God and my faith in that power. When things get really tough, I can bend down and sip from those waters, gaining a renewed strength. I'm helped by a comparison to life a few years back. Then the well was dry—nothing but a black, awful pit that swallowed me whole and left me with nowhere to go. I thank God I now have somewhere to go."

I was still talking to Tracy on the phone once in awhile. We'd quit seeing each other because I'd finally accepted the fact that personal visits only intensified the strong emotional ties I had with her and brought up physical temptations. I had reached the point where I spent very little time thinking about her or other women in inappropriate ways.

Treating myself kindly was an important change, too. I began to love and accept myself, weaknesses and all. I spent my weekends doing whatever I wanted, as long as it was within the Lord's boundaries. Previously, my only sources of happiness were outside those boundaries, so I had some re-learning to do.

I felt like a kid as I visited national parks and reserves and zoos and museums and mountains and beaches. I took a camera with me everywhere. I loved the creativity and positive energy that photography brought into my life. It was, quite literally, a whole new world for me. I began to be fed by the Spirit as I learned to meet my needs righteously.

I wanted a life with Christ. I didn't want the alternative. And I began to see that the choice had to be made. I knew I could not love two masters.

Temple covenants help put off the natural man.

After a time of increased faith, repentance, and obedience to the commandments, I felt ready to talk to my bishop about the possibility of receiving the temple endowment. Because I'd moved again, I needed to meet with another bishop. I gave him a brief overview of my past, my current situation, and why I felt ready to go to the temple. As we talked, I was astounded that together we determined the only thing I needed to do was turn in some unpaid tithing and I'd be worthy to enter the House of the Lord.

It was difficult for me to fully grasp that reality. A judge in Israel had declared my worthiness to participate in some of the holiest ordinances on earth.

Now, the challenge was for me to *feel* clean and worthy.

I struggled to feel worthy because, without realizing it, I was depending upon my own merits. I knew the Savior suffered and died for my sins. All of them. The serious ones and the not-so-serious ones. But I wasn't sure how I could be completely forgiven for *everything*. I'd lived so many years with sin, guilt, shame, suicidal thoughts, sinful desires, addictions, doubt, confusion, trauma, guilt, turmoil, self-hatred, anger toward God, mistrust, resentment, regret, and isolation. How could I let all that go when it seemed like part of me, who I really was? How could I ever forgive myself?

By thinking I wasn't doing enough to become worthy, I was trying to purify myself. I failed to realize that I could not do it by myself. Certainly I had to do the work, but only Jesus Christ can cleanse and purify. In the eternal scheme of things, it is His forgiveness that truly matters. My opinion is nothing more than that: a mortal's opinion, which pales in comparison and can certainly be off the mark.

I prayed for, and soon received, an undeniable witness that my Savior, Jesus Christ, had cleansed me from sin and the negative emotions attached to it. I accepted the fact that all of my sins had truly been washed away.

I was clean and spotless.

I had been made pure, changed from the deepest crimson to bright white. All because Christ fulfilled the law and suffered "pains and afflictions and temptations of every kind."[7] He experienced all that could happen to mortals. He faced a depth and breadth of agony that no mortal could possibly fathom—the "awful arithmetic of the Atonement."[8] Voluntarily, He bled from every pore and drank the bitter cup. He suffered on the cross until it was finished.

There was no doubt as to whom I was eternally indebted. And to think I had been healed so miraculously that I could commit to obey the Word of Wisdom and live the law of chastity, with confidence.

My profound gratitude for His sacrifices and suffering on my behalf helped motivate me to avoid further sin. I did not want to be the cause of greater suffering for Him.

It seemed important for me to attend the temple weekly after receiving my endowment, so I did. I quickly learned that temple work may redeem the dead, but it also has incredible power to redeem the living.

During that first year, I went to ten different temples. I enjoyed traveling, so I would plan a trip around a U.S. city where a temple was located. I loved all the things unique to each temple. Like the stars carved into the celestial room's glass windows at the Las Vegas temple, forming stars of light on the carpet when the sun shines through at just the right angle. And the sound of the crystal pieces gently touching each other on the chandelier in the Washington D.C. temple, creating a light tinkling of various pitches softly harmonizing, like the whispering of angels. The incredible reliefs on the ceiling of the celestial room in the Salt Lake temple. Historic paintings in various rooms of the Manti temple and its live sessions.

In each temple, I also found comforting and reassuring similarities, too. Like the purity and strength of the spirit. The power of the endowment session to clear my mind of life's concerns so I could be left with a miraculously pure and holy mindset. The kindness and charity emanating from the people who worked there as they greeted me with warm, welcoming smiles and provided holy assistance. I didn't feel judged, or out of place, or like I was viewing a moving diorama. I felt like an integral part of what was taking place within those hallowed walls.

Everyone wore white, so fashions of the day and social distinctions disappeared. My years of sinful living and my desire to go back disappeared, too. I marvelled as I heard, again and again, the blessings of the washing and anointing.

I also noticed how persistently and craftily the adversary works to keep us out of the temple. It was often the small things–running behind with work, feeling tired, having no gas in the car–that almost kept me away. I still managed to keep my weekly commitment because I knew it was important, for many reasons.

Best of all, there was a sense of home. A heavenly home. The feeling was usually fleeting, yet undeniable. It was as if the veil had fluttered open in the breeze, carrying a familiar scent of home–melancholic in its absence, reassuring in its presence and glory.

I had experienced something similar at other times, usually in the fall. Autumn leaves, campfires, pumpkins, a big pot of chili–the familiar scent of home. "All things on earth point home in old October."[9]

Just two months after going through the temple for the first time, I felt impressed to start writing a book to help others with challenges similar to mine. I'd frequently been frustrated by the fact that I had nothing to read that directly helped with my journey. I criticized "the Church" because "they" hadn't written anything helping with homosexuality.

At some point, I realized that the "they" I was criticizing included me as a Church member. If I felt strongly that there should be a book, perhaps I should write it.

Although I didn't know it at the time, my writing would be cathartic and deepen my understanding of God, the world, and myself. It would change my life mightily, in ways that I never thought possible. My testimony was further strengthened as I studied, searched, and pondered the scriptures in an effort to know what I should write.

I was amazed at the strength and Light that I found by searching the scriptures for hours every day and making sacramental and temple covenants every week. I drew unto Jesus Christ in new ways. I discovered that the temple held great cleansing power—not just cleansing from sin but also from pain and anger and all the rest of it.

The Light and knowledge I continued to receive in the temple helped uncover the darkness and weaknesses I still held within. I was able to recognize and deal with issues at a deeper level. The process was so important because it helped me release that which still held me bound to sinful desires.

It was a somewhat tumultuous time, too. On occasion, inappropriate desires became stronger than they had been in years. I found remnants that remained at a deeper level. I also discovered more anger and guilt from the abuse and from my homosexual attractions. It took determination and divine assistance to get me through. I used all the strength I had. I'm certain I could not have withstood the force of those temptations and desires any earlier.

As I did all I could to rid myself of unrighteous desires and whatever they were attached to, those desires were removed through the divine grace and healing power of Jesus Christ. I uprooted, worked through, and cast off the leftover junk with help from a good friend, a professional therapist, and writing. As usual, the greatest personal changes came through the power of the Atonement.

Searching for help through stormy times.

I hadn't told anyone in the new singles ward I attended about my past or about the book I was working on because I was afraid of being judged. Even though I wasn't involved in a lesbian relationship or breaking the Word of Wisdom, that was still part of my past, and also my present since I was writing about it. There was still a stigma attached to homosexuality and substance abuse. That stigma exists today, although it has definitely improved.

As the burden of the book became more than I could bear without support from friends, I finally decided to open up to a friend of mine from Church. She started fidgeting around when I told her, even though I kept the discussion as vague and inoffensive as possible. I mentioned that, in an effort to help others, I spoke with Latter-day Saints who were still dealing with homosexuality on a daily basis.

"That's sick."

I can still hear those words and feel the pain. I guess she thought that because I wasn't currently involved, I wouldn't take it personally. Or, maybe she just didn't think.

Regardless, my heart sank. When she said, "That's sick" she might as well have said, "You're sick for having been involved in that stuff!" Her body language reiterated the same message. It became so uncomfortable I had to leave.

I went home feeling devastated. I thought maybe the whole idea of working on the book was ridiculous. Maybe I was just some sicko unable to think straight. I quit writing and studying the scriptures that week. I felt dejected, even ashamed for no good reason.

Late one night, while I was in the middle of praying to know what to do, I was startled by a knock at the door. It was my Relief Society president.

Dana was a great person, but she didn't seem like the kind of woman I would be good friends with. I thought she was so Molly Mormonesque, if I dare confess to being so judgmental. She came from a family of 11, all BYU graduates, returned missionaries, temple marriages, the works. She was extremely feminine in appearance and actions and spoke with a very soft, kind voice. She reminded me of, well, a Relief Society president. That made me uneasy. I still didn't feel all that comfortable at Relief Society, nor did I feel like I fit in very well.

So, when Dana said she felt like there was something bothering me and she wanted to help, I laughed inside at the thought of disclosing to her. I'd disclosed to a friend I knew well and the results were disastrous. I certainly wasn't going to make that mistake again, especially not with a "typical

Mormon." As we continued to talk, the spirit prompted me to tell her all about what was going on. I ignored the prompting, dismissing it as my imagination. Then I felt it again. And again.

I finally launched into the whole story, telling her all about my background, the book I had been writing, and why I'd been writing it. I thought for sure she'd have no idea what to say and would quickly find a reason to leave. My judgments were misplaced.

Instead of using the word "sick" as I feared she might, she used words like "strong," "faithful," "perseverant" and "impressive." She spoke of her admiration for me because I had dealt with great challenges, turned everything around, and was now working to help others. She was simply and compassionately Christlike in her response. The spirit bore strong witness as she spoke. I knew the Lord had brought her to my doorstep.

Dana was just what I needed to continue the work. She became a remarkable support and a very dear friend through it all. I certainly could not have finished the book without all of her help.

The touch of the Master's hand.

One evening while working on the book, I became discouraged again. It seemed like I was never going to finish writing it. I began to question, again, whether or not I was up for the task. It presented such great challenges and it required so much from me, I wasn't sure I could follow it through to completion.

I reread my life story at the beginning of the book, for the umpteenth time. Then I came to the journal entry I'd written:

> Dear God, it's black again.
> Two solid months of darkness.
> Two solid days of light marked Christ's arrival.
>
> I guess He isn't coming.
>
> Have faith, you say?
> But faith does not hold my hand.
> Or stroke my hair and tell me I'm OK.

Just as I read that, something, or someone, stroked my hair. I was overcome with the Spirit, physically as well as spiritually. I realized, in a powerful new way, that I was loved and that the Savior was there for me. I wish I could express how real it was—express the incredible feelings of peace and comfort and love undefiled.

I know that my Redeemer lives. He came to my aid that evening.

Mighty changes and becoming spiritually reborn.

The process of putting off the natural man, becoming spiritually reborn and filled with the love of Christ was greatly accelerated through temple attendance, intense scripture study, and writing the book. Up until that point, my goal had been to sacrifice homosexual relationships, drugs, and alcohol before I died. I'd figured that was my life's mission.

Apparently, it was just the beginning.

I became aware of more things I needed to sacrifice. I gave up a high-paying job to find one that would give me more time to come unto Christ and work on the book. I stopped seeing R-rated movies. I quit drinking Diet Coke. I devoted more of my time, energy and talents to the building up of The Church of Jesus Christ of Latter-day Saints. And just when I'd reached a point where I could be perfectly happy sitting on a mountaintop watching the breeze go by, I was asked to sacrifice much of my free time to serve others.

Fortunately, sacrifice after sacrifice brought forth blessing after blessing.

One day Dana and I spent hours going through Glenn L. Pace's book, *Spiritual Plateaus*. In it he describes the process of the mighty change and sanctification, something both of us had been interested in. We took turns reading the book aloud and marking it with Post-it Notes. I still have that book, filled with ragged sticky notes and the inscription that Dana wrote on the inside cover, "A time of spiritual stretching."

Glenn L. Pace states, "Sometimes we overlook the fact that a spiritual transformation or metamorphosis must take place within us. It comes about through grace and by the Spirit of God, although it does not come about until we have truly repented and proven ourselves worthy. We can be guilty of being so careful to live the letter of the law that we don't develop our inner spiritual nature and fine-tune our spiritual communication to the point that we may receive sanctification and purification. My conclusion is that we will not be saved by works if those works are not born of a disposition to do good, as opposed to an obligation to do good."[10]

He goes on to explain how the process of sanctification, a mighty change in desires, and the resultant disposition to do good come about and the steps we need to take.

I was fascinated by the whole concept and felt that was what I stood in need of. So, I applied the steps he discussed, including introspection, scripture study, obedience, acting upon impulses to do good and praying for sanctification.

I was impressed by Elder Pace's suggestion that we use trials as stepping stones rather than stumbling blocks in order to increase spirituality. That way we can experience sanctification "geometrically, accelerating the process of the mighty change through trials."[11]

I began to reconsider my trials and think of new ways in which I could respond to them so I could use them as stepping stones. I pondered this, especially while in the temple.

During one temple session, I felt I needed to sacrifice what had become a mostly distant friendship with Tracy. It didn't really make sense. I rarely spoke with her. We simply talked as friends. But since I'd already learned that impressions trump common sense, I acted on it.

I called Tracy that night to have a difficult conversation.

She didn't understand why we couldn't still be friends. After all, we hadn't done anything inappropriate for years. I didn't know what to tell her. All I kept saying was that I was so sorry but it seemed like the right thing to do.

She felt terrible. I felt terrible. We had worked so hard to reach the point where we could be friends. Why should that have to stop?

Then, quite unexpectedly and unknowingly, I said, "I'm still in love with you."

We were both surprised that I said it. Then I started to cry, "I'm sorry I can't just be friends. I'm sorry, but I don't know how to quit being in love with you."

Tracy and I had shared so much and genuinely cared about each other. With the inappropriateness aside, there was a great deal of Christlike love there. But apparently, I hadn't put all of the inappropriate feelings aside. Although they were hidden, and not acted upon nor even fantasized about for years, there was still a part of me that was in love with a woman.

Worthy to enter the temple? Yes. Able to be purified and sanctified? Not with that feeling still keeping me connected to that part of our relationship.

After I hung up with Tracy, I knelt in prayer. I offered up the friendship and my feelings of still being in love with her. As I did, I sensed a change in how I felt. It's nothing I can describe, but a definite change was occurring. I literally felt something in my heart and chest.

The room became lighter, or at least it seemed that way.

I continued to pray and my words became a narration of what seemed to be taking place. It was like the words were being put into my mouth as I described how I was partaking of the fruit of the love of God and how it was delicious and most desirable and joyous to my soul.

The best description comes from a scriptural passage I hadn't previously equated with sanctification and the mighty change of heart:

"I did go forth and partake of the fruit thereof; and I beheld that it was most sweet, above all that I ever before tasted. Yea, and I beheld that the fruit thereof was white, to exceed all the whiteness that I had ever seen. And as I partook of the fruit thereof it filled my soul with exceedingly great joy." [12]

Nephi explains what it represents: "Yea, it is the love of God, which sheddeth itself abroad in the hearts of the children of men; wherefore, it is the most desirable above all things...Yea, and the most joyous to the soul." [13]

When I finished praying, the whole room seemed even brighter. As strange as it might sound (and I'd never really known what this meant before), I truly wished to sing a song of redeeming love. I had been redeemed, after all.

Ever since then, it has been impossible for me to fool myself into thinking that anything is more desirous than partaking of the pure love of God. I've made plenty of other mistakes, for sure. But I have never again chosen to pursue a forbidden path rather than follow the strait and narrow.

Studying and pondering the concept of the mighty

change no doubt facilitated the process as I worked on the manuscript for *Born That Way.*

Little did I know that as I was finishing up the book on that part of my life, a new chapter was just beginning.

{ Creating a Temple Marriage }
MIGHTY CHANGE III

After *Born That Way* was published, I knew that I'd never be able to completely bury my past. It was bound to pop up somewhere, landing on some ward member's nightstand or a neighbor's bookshelf. Probably where I least expected it. I used a pen name but still, there would be no hiding my life story from anyone I was close to, not to mention total strangers.

I was also fairly certain the book would eliminate my already slim chances of meeting a "nice Mormon man" that I'd want to marry. Of course, I frequently considered that to be an added bonus.

I liked most men just fine. Falling in love with one, however, was an entirely different matter. At the time I received my temple endowment, I was pretty sure my commitment to live the law of chastity was a commitment to remain celibate for the rest of my life. I had lived the alternative with women and it didn't work for me.

My attraction to the gospel proved to be stronger than my attraction to women.

While writing the manuscript, I did start making more of an effort to date men (leaps of faith, to be sure). That brought up different issues. Dana suggested I read the book *One Flesh, One Heart* by LDS marriage and family therapist, Dr. Carlfred Broderick. He had become the department chair of sociology at USC and executive director of their Marriage and Family Therapy Training Program.

While reading Dr. Broderick's book, I was especially struck by the passage where he discussed men who had come to him with homosexual struggles. Some of what he described, I had experienced:

"At first, the possibility of ever being back on the track to the kingdom with a temple marriage and normal lifestyle seemed so far away to them that they could only contemplate it with despair. But, step-by-step, they reached that goal. First, they learned how to deal with their negative feelings toward themselves. Gradually, they came to realize that they were of worth, whatever their life-style or afflictions. Next, they learned to conform to the commandments, even if only in a mechanical way. By the time they were living worthy to go to the temple, the Lord began to work a mighty change in their hearts. In each case, separately, they began to dream romantically about women and to discover the stirrings of attraction toward the opposite sex while losing feelings of attraction toward their own. Next, for each, the Lord raised up a good, patient woman who loved well and was easy to love in return. As each has said, 'This has been a series of miracles!'

"The key is in the word 'series'... By contrast, those who prayed, however fervently, for the miracle from the beginning never received it, and if they were not willing to try the experiment of faith, step by step, they became bitter against

God for his refusal to answer them and turned again to their former lifestyle."[1]

I'd already dealt with my negative feelings toward myself, realized I was of worth, learned to conform to the commandments, and became worthy to enter the temple. I began to wonder if the rest might be possible, too.

Dr. Broderick lived in Southern California, not too far from where I lived, so I called to set up a therapy session. When we met, we discussed gospel principles and how I'd been applying them to my life, my struggles, and to the manuscript for *Born That Way*.

Just before I was about to leave, he stood up and announced: "I cannot, in good conscience, charge you for today or any other day. This is not therapy. It's gospel study. Call me when you need to and we'll meet at USC."

He became more animated as he spoke. "This is divine providence. Who am I to stand in the way?"

Dr. Broderick and my friend Dana were more evidence of how the Lord kept putting people in my life – just the people I needed, right when I needed them. Bishop Garey and Leeza came into my life when I needed them, too. Their love, acceptance, and support made all the difference. More irrefutable evidence that "the Lord giveth no commandments unto the children of men, save he shall prepare a way for them that they may accomplish the thing which he commandeth them."[2]

Dr. Broderick was brilliant, well-read, *and* well-written, with a bachelor's degree from Harvard and a PhD from Cornell. He had been a bishop and a stake president, eventually being called as patriarch. I think he was working on his twelfth book when I first met him. He liked to say he'd written as many books as he had grandchildren.

Few mental health professionals were as knowledgeable *and* as spiritually grounded as Dr. Broderick. Several times, while slogging through my past in order to finish the manuscript, I'd experience intense feelings for women or a desire to escape through drugs and alcohol. I'd go in to Carlfred – in a panic – and say something like, "See, I haven't changed! I'm never going to change!"

He'd calm me down and talk some spiritual sense into me. "Don't tell me you haven't changed. Of course you have! You aren't having sex with women. You aren't fantasizing about them. You aren't drinking or abusing drugs. You're a worthy temple recommend holder. I'd say that's change, wouldn't you?"

He always had a way of helping me step back from my intense, confusing feelings in order to correct my distorted thinking using eternal truths. Fortunately, at that point in my life, I was far enough along that I *could* step back and separate myself from my attractions and desires to commit serious sins.

Carlfred also bore powerful witness to me, time and time again, that I only had to identify as gay or alcoholic if I chose to identify as such. "You are a chosen daughter of God, my dear. That's who you are. I am a professional psychologist who is perfectly capable of helping gays and lesbians who want to live that life. But it's obvious you are far more interested in living the gospel of Jesus Christ. Is that not true?"

He was one part lawyer, one part storyteller, one part therapist, and seven parts spiritual leader.

"Tell me," he continued, "do you want to be sealed in the temple, to a man?"

"Can I have some time to think about it?" The thought still made me uncomfortable. The few guys I'd dated I liked. It was the transition into something more serious that created the difficulties.

"Take all the time you need. Believe me, if you're meant to marry in this life, you'll be given the desire to do so. The Lord asks you to remain faithful and to believe marriage is a possibility. He doesn't expect you to produce attractions on your own. He helps create your desires."

"Well, since I'm willing to date single Mormon guys over the age of 30, that means I'm showing a whole lot of faith, right?" I spoke rather smugly.

"Sure. As long as they are willing to date a single Mormon *gal* over the age of 30." Carlfred was usually quicker with a comeback than I was.

Signs and wonders.

My life seemed to change every time I turned around. Perhaps to prove that I could fit into Relief Society, or maybe just to show He has a sense of humor, the Lord called me to be Relief Society president.

I was stunned. I was sure that I was as far from Relief Society president material as a person could get. But I also knew the Lord had called me. I certainly wasn't the logical choice, or the obvious one, so I had to be the inspired one.

That calling helped me grow in ways I never predicted. The first time I walked into the Relief Society room after being set apart, I was filled with incomprehensible love for every woman in there. The love seemed to fill the room and spill over.

I stood all amazed.

There I was in a roomful of Relief Society sisters, much like the roomful of sisters I'd walked into when I first returned to activity in the Church. Back then it felt so foreign, like the diorama I was viewing from the outside. But with the mantle of president, I felt a part of a group of women in a whole new way.

There was nothing inappropriate about my love for those women. I felt safe with my feelings for them and not concerned that it might be something else. There was no need to keep my guard up, or to be nervous about my feelings because they were an extension of the mantle and the pure love of Christ. It was a purity I hadn't known before, and I came to cherish it.

Not long after I was called as Relief Society president, I met Dallas. He'd come to our ward with Mark, a mutual friend of ours. While I talked to him, I thought, "Gee, this guy's good looking, nice, smart, 37 years old and single. I wonder what's wrong with him?" (Ignoring the fact that something might be wrong with me, of course.)

When I got the chance, I asked Mark.

"Nothing's wrong with him. He just started coming back to Church. And he's single because he doesn't date all that much."

Dallas had been raised in the LDS Church, but he'd quit attending a few years after returning home from his mission. He was too smart for his own good. His personal creed was an altered scripture he'd heard somewhere:

"All we like cats have gone astray."

He deemed it more appropriate to compare his wandering from the fold to a cat going astray rather than a dimwitted sheep. Having grown up on a farm, he said that sheep are dumb animals. He insisted he was not like some dopey sheep, aimlessly wandering about. Instead, he was like the clever, curious cat looking for something new and intellectually challenging.

After his mission, he'd decided to put away childish things and start thinking of religion as an adult. So off he went, with catlike curiosity, to discover real answers. Trouble was, the more he looked for logical explanations, the less sense his life seemed to make.

Over the years, he managed to become quite lost. Sheep, cat, hippopotamus, pterodactyl—no matter what he wanted to call himself, he was still lost. And his only hope for rescue was the Good Shepherd.

One Sunday, at the home of his cousin, Dale, his 4-year-old daughter invited him to go to church with them. Dallas could not resist her innocence and childlike faith, so he joined the family for church. That was enough to get him to go to church a few more times, and that's when I met him.

Mark was convinced Dallas and I should go out, so he set up a double date. After that, Dallas called to ask me to lunch. It wasn't so much a date. More like a couple of friends grabbing a bite to eat. I could handle that. I had neither the time nor the inclination to start a relationship with a man that didn't seem too interested in the Church. I was busy writing about unwanted homosexual desires, and I had a self-imposed manuscript deadline to meet.

"The Mormon Church really ought to be a democracy," Dallas declared over the top of his pastrami and sauerkraut sandwich.

"The Church, a democracy?" I laughed out loud. "That's a great idea! Let's put all the commandments up for vote. I vote we quit going to church on Sundays and start enjoying a second weekend day like everyone else. What commandments would you vote down?"

He looked at me with furrowed brow. I knew that wasn't where he was headed with the conversation. I was just playing angel's advocate.

We continued the back and forth as if we were playing an intense game of tennis, with a really long rally. That remained our favorite sport for quite some time. Dallas would express his intellectual and political objections to the LDS Church. Then I'd defend it based on gospel principles. Not to mention a heavy dose of sarcasm.

Dallas liked that I wasn't intimidated by his intellectual firepower. Normally I would have been, if it were just a battle of wits. He was extremely well-read, whereas I'd never gotten much further than *Where the Red Fern Grows* and *To Kill a Mockingbird*. However, I wielded the sword of truth with a fair amount of swordsmanship, mostly because I'd spent the past few years researching and writing the book. That entailed prayerful searching of scriptures, conference addresses, and related literature. I was prepared to do battle with the best of naysayers, and Dallas was among the best.

Dallas' intellectualism and dissection of the Church also helped me feel safe in our relationship. I figured I didn't have to worry about getting too serious because if I ever got married – a big if, to be sure – it would be in the temple. Certainly Dallas wouldn't want to marry in the temple. And why should I bother with anything else after I'd gone to so much trouble to become temple-worthy?

A conference address reminded me of Dallas and his struggles with the gospel, so I read it to him. Elder Glenn L. Pace quotes Elder James E. Faust when he talks about Latter-day Saints who intellectualize specific issues after they've already joined the Church.

"Elder Faust describes this type of intellectual as 'a person who continues to chase after a bus even after he has caught it.' We invite everyone to get on the bus before it's out of sight and you are left forever trying to figure out the infinite with a finite mind."[3]

On the way home from a minor league baseball game one evening, Dallas told me he was taking an analytical approach to the Book of Mormon, examining it for its historical merit. He commented that after he first began reading, he had a strange notion he should pray to see whether or not the Book of Mormon was true. But he cast the idea aside and kept on reading.

"I need to read the whole book before I can determine its merits."

I slugged him in the shoulder (so much for gentle persuasion). "For such a smart guy, you sure can be a dope sometimes! Knowledge – true spiritual knowledge – can't be found through intellectual reasoning. Perfect knowledge only comes through faith, and only after it has been nourished like a seed and allowed to sprout and swell and grow.

You haven't made it to Alma 32 yet, have you?"

He took my sarcasm in stride. "I told you I barely started the book before I thought I should pray about it. I didn't even make it out of First Nephi."

"Use your brains to your advantage, not your demise." I let out half a laugh.

"You're sure of yourself, aren't you?" he challenged.

"No, I'm not sure of myself. The one thing I *am* sure about is the gospel of Jesus Christ." The spirit punctuated my statement with such strength, it took both of us by surprise.

I continued, "Even our intellect is affected by the fall. If we simply try to reason things out, then we'll end up with flawed human reasoning."

I had a tough time explaining what I meant. A couple of years later, I found a Steven Robinson quote where he'd done a good job explaining it in his book, *Following Christ:*

"We have a tendency to think that if we start with what we know to be true and proceed with correct logic, we will always arrive at correct conclusions, but that is wrong, for human reason is flawed–it is fallen. Fallen intellect can't get things right…

"Those who rely on intellect and human reasoning alone as their surest guides in this life are doomed to be 'ever learning but never able to come to a knowledge of the truth.'"[4]

After a few more outings together, Dallas and I took a trip to Lake Arrowhead to meet some friends. On the way there, he started talking about the Church. However, the more he spoke, the more he lost his sharp, cutting edge.

Then he opened up about his struggles with his faith. It was not his usual deconstruction of the gospel.

As we traveled up the mountain pass, I had a feeling we should pull over and pray. I wasn't sure how Dallas would react, so I didn't say anything. It was dark, and a fairly dense fog grew thicker the further up we drove.

The impression to pray became more urgent until I could no longer ignore the still, small, persistent voice.

"Hey, would you mind if we pulled over to pray? I keep feeling like we should."

"Sure, if we can find a place to pull over."

The turnouts were difficult to see because of the fog. We finally found a spot where we could pull over, just as the thick fog pressed up against the car and reduced our visibility to next to nothing.

I offered to say the prayer so Dallas wouldn't feel put on the spot. I started out using the typical prayer-speak as filler while I desperately thought of what to say. It seemed important, so I wanted to be sure to follow inspiration.

At some point, I quit thinking on my own and started paying attention to the Spirit. Next thing I knew, the prayer turned into one of those communions with heaven that takes on a life of its own.

I did my best to keep pace.

Dallas and I felt united in prayer as I pled for divine assistance so he could hear and follow the guidance of the Holy Spirit. I called upon the powers of heaven to help him see Truth and recognize the correct path that lay before him on the plain road.

While we were praying, a wind apparently came up and

cleared the fog away. Dallas started the car. When he turned on the headlights, we looked up to see, just a few feet in front of us, a big green reflective highway sign. Its bold white letters were shining brightly back at us. The sign simply read: "Mormon Road."

Apparently the sign marked an old lumber road built by early Mormon settlers in the San Bernardino Valley.

We stared at that sign, then looked at each other and started to laugh. We kept on laughing, and every time one of us tried to speak, we started laughing again.

I finally managed to get out a few words. "Signs only come by faith, you know. And a little help from the Department of Transportation."

That sign was never forgotten. Even though we always laughed about it, the humor carried with it an unspoken faith that served to underpin our relationship with each other and with God. We both knew that the prayer and the presence of that sign were not coincidental.

Heavenly Father has used humor to help strengthen my faith on numerous occasions. In fact, while Dallas and I were still dating, we attended a session of general conference in the tabernacle. On the way there, we had a talk about repentance and change. It was a hot, sunny day and many of us sitting in the balcony were fanning ourselves. President Hinckley was conducting. He looked up toward us and said, with his wonderful sense of humor, "Now you know what it will feel like if you don't repent."

The more time I spent with Dallas, the more I enjoyed his company. There was a problem, however. Even though I thought he was nice looking, for a guy, I had no desire to be physically intimate with him, in any way. In addition to the fact he was a man, his large stature put me on edge. Dallas was 6'4", about 200 pounds, with an athletic build.

Not that I really thought about it consciously, but the other guys I'd dated weren't much bigger than I was. In therapy, I realized that was because I felt safer. If a guy ever "wanted his way with me," I could fight him off, as long as I didn't freeze up.

I tactfully avoided any subtle advances from Dallas, which were few and far between. That was something else I appreciated about him. He was shy and reserved with such matters, and didn't pressure me to kiss him.

I could tell he was attracted to me, and that made me nervous. I just wanted to be friends. I liked it that way.

Then came the fateful night at my apartment.

That fateful night.

"So I was wondering," Dallas said to me one evening, "I was wondering if you might be interested in, uh, the 'r' thing."

"The 'r' thing?" I had no idea what he meant.

"You know, the 'r' thing."

His nervousness was making *me* nervous, so I tried comic relief. "You mean rhubarb pie?"

"No, not rhubarb pie. I was wondering if you might be interested in a relationship, with me. I was hoping you and I could become more serious."

Curses! I figured such a time was likely coming, but I was still caught off guard. And at a loss for words, which wasn't like me.

Finally I said, "Dallas, I really enjoy your company. I like you, I do. But as far as a serious relationship goes, we're headed in two different directions."

"Why do you say that?"

"Well, you attack the Church. I defend it."

"So?"

"If I ever get married, it's going to be in the temple. I've worked far too hard to settle for anything else."

"What makes you think I don't want the same thing?"

He was indignant.

I was shocked.

"You want to get married in the temple? Really?"

"Is that so hard to believe?"

"Well, since you constantly criticize the Church."

"Maybe I'm looking for someone to defend it. Maybe I care more than you think."

The double entendre did not go unnoticed. He'd pulled the safety net right out from under me. All this time I'd been so sure I was safe doing things with him. I wouldn't have to worry about a serious relationship because he wasn't serious about the gospel. I had hoped a physical attraction might develop over time, but it hadn't–despite how much I was attracted to him in other ways.

Panic set in. My heart started racing, and not in a good way. I was at a loss for words, yet again.

The silence grew in length, becoming more and more awkward. I knew we were both waiting for me to say something. That's when an idea popped into my head. An idea that sheer desperation must have conjured up.

"Just a minute. Let me get something."

I walked over to my desk, picked up the manuscript for *Born That Way,* and walked back over to Dallas. Then I took all 142 pages, filled with the worst sins I had ever committed, and plopped them down in his lap.

"Here, read this. If you still want a relationship when you're done, then we'll talk."

He stared down at the 142 pages with a puzzled look on his face, and then looked back up at me. "What's this?"

By now, all the blood had drained from my body and gone heaven knows where. I thought I was going to pass out. I knew I had to get him out of there, fast.

"It's sort of like a journal. A really *long* journal." I was stammering, not sure how to answer him. I didn't want to reveal anything, to his face.

"Actually, it's uhhhh, a manuscript for a book that I wrote. And Deseret Book is going to publish it."

"Really?" He sounded impressed.

"Before you get too impressed, you should read it."

He started glancing through the pages. I reached over and slammed them back down in the pile, much faster and harder than I meant to. "No, not now!"

Dallas gave me a puzzled look.

I didn't want to be anywhere near him when he read all about my past. I'd already faced more than my share of rejection in my life.

I was grateful I'd already planned a camping trip for the weekend with a few friends from Church.

"I'll tell you what. I'm going camping with friends this weekend. You read the manuscript while I'm gone. Then if you still want that rhubarb pie thing, you can meet me here for dinner at 6:00 Sunday night. If you don't show, I'll understand. You don't even need to call."

I saw no reason to be verbally rejected, too.

He held up the ream of paper that was the manuscript. "I'm supposed to read all this by Sunday?" He laughed as he shook his head.

"You're a fast reader. It'll just take you a couple of hours, I'm sure."

"Right. I'll see you Sunday then."

"Maybe." I gestured toward the doorway, doing all I could to refrain myself from physically pushing him out the door.

"Go on," I insisted. "I promise you'll understand more when you read it."

Yeah, he'd understand more all right. Like why I wouldn't let him kiss me. And why I was still single. And why I clung so tightly to the iron rod as the mists of darkness swirled about. And why I defended the Church like the fully outfitted, totally dedicated defender of Truth I had become.

I'd already told him there was a long period of time I didn't go to church. I'd alluded to my past use of drugs and alcohol. However, I'd only revealed the tip of the iceberg–an iceberg large enough to sink the Titanic. Not to mention a relationship.

Stories round the campfire.

The next evening, I was the source of entertainment around the campfire. All three of my camping pals had been supportive of my past, my manuscript, and me. Except that evening. They were having way too much fun.

"I can't believe you just plopped that big ol' manuscript in his lap without so much as a warning."

"You just wanted to scare him off."

"That's one way out."

"No, I think she really likes him. Look, she's blushing."

I couldn't get a word in edgewise. Plus, I honestly wasn't sure if I'd given him the manuscript to scare him off or to draw him in. Perhaps I was letting fate decide.

"It's dark. You can't tell if I'm blushing or not!" I protested the only point I was sure I could protest.

Just thinking about Dallas reading my life story put butterflies in my stomach—or maybe moths trying to eat their way out. I wasn't sure whether or not I wanted him to show up on Sunday.

I knew I'd be quite sad if I couldn't spend time with him anymore. Then again, if he showed up after knowing everything about me, what excuse could I use in order to break off the relationship?

Did I want an excuse?

And if I didn't have one, and I couldn't rationalize a breakup, surely he'd expect to kiss me. That's what folks do when they're in a "relationship," or a "rhubarb pie."

What would I do then?

"To be honest," I announced, "I'm not sure how I feel about it all."

I picked up a marshmallow and busied myself positioning it on the end of the stick, just so, in order to roast it to a nice, even brown. I just wanted to think about roasting marshmallows. That I could control. Sort of.

"No wonder you wanted to go camping. Are you sure we're far enough away from Dallas?" Julie knew me all too well. She knew I was trying to escape the conversation with a marshmallow.

"We had this trip planned before I decided to dump the manuscript in his lap. Before he said he wanted the 'rhubarb pie' thing."

"You two are meant for each other," Julie announced. "Neither one of you can even say the word. C'mon, try. Ree-lay-shun-ship!"

"Very funny."

"Aren't you dying of curiosity. Dallas is probably reading all about your life as we speak."

"Thanks for reminding me, Julie."

"Will he stay or will he go?" (*Julie singing solo, grotesquely out of tune.*)

"Will he stay or will he go!" (*Trio of friends singing, out of tune times three.*)

"There's nothing like the support of my dear friends in my time of need."

Just then my marshmallow burst into flames. I pulled it out from the coals and didn't bother to blow it out. I just watched it burn. I'd lost my appetite anyway.

I spent the rest of the trip trying not to think about what might be going on back in civilization. Of course, my dear friends kept reminding me.

Mighty changes.

Sunday at 6:00 was torturously slow in coming.

5:32. Tick, tick, tick.

5:32. Same as the last time I looked.

Whether it was sheer optimism or utter stupidity, I cannot say. But I'd gotten this big slab of London broil to cook up for the Sunday dinner. It would have been too much food if Dallas *did* show. And if he didn't? No doubt I'd feel that much more alone sitting at a candlelit table, all by myself, with enough meat to feed Helaman's army.

5:59. He's not coming or he'd be here by now. It's just as well.

6:01. He really isn't coming, which is just fine by me. Maybe I won't ever have to worry about trying to like some guy again. I can just get on with my single life. It's easier that way.

6:02. Knock, knock.

Gasp.

I hesitated before I opened the door so I wouldn't seem too anxious.

Dallas stood on the front step and held his place. He looked at me, teared up, and then reached forward to place his hand on my shoulder.

Something was different about him. He seemed, softer. Even his face had changed somehow. He looked different.

I realized it was his countenance that had changed.

As he stepped across the threshold, I let my guard down. His countenance, his presence, and his depth of soul–I found the combination to be magnetizing. It was all manifest in such a tangible way.

I felt myself drawn in as a natural response.

We reached for each other and embraced, as if we had done it a million times before. I didn't feel threatened by his strength. The opposite was true. I felt protected while he enfolded me in his arms.

It wasn't the same kind of safety I'd experienced with women. This was different somehow. And the fact that he was a man suddenly wasn't an issue. Even his scent, with a hint of masculinity, drew me to him. It carried an odd sense of familiarity, like when you smell a scent that you haven't smelled in years and you're immediately transported to a place back in time. Only this was like I was being transported back and forward at the same time.

I'd never been physically attracted to him before. But now, everything about him seemed native to me–his solid arms, chest and shoulders. The gentleness of his strength.

"I'm sorry. I am so sorry you had to go through all of that and I wasn't there to protect you." He cried as he spoke.

I even loved the softness of his deep, rich voice.

We looked at each other.

The silence spoke volumes.

He held me close again. As we stood there, entwined, it was difficult to tell where he ended and I began. I felt aroused, not in the typical sexual way. This was different. It was intensely spiritual and emotional, even physical, but in a way I'd never experienced before.

Words fall short. All of them. Love, comfort, healing, acceptance, companionship, eternal marriage, blessed, steadiness, truth, godhood, passion, rapture, peace, calm.

Every confusion of identity or concern about romantic attractions for a man seemed to spontaneously combust. A baptism of fire.

Other feelings seemed to go up in flames as well. Fear,

guilt, shame, mistrust, confusion, want for a woman, want for an escape, want for a life contrary to God's life.

All of it, all at once, across an entire lifetime. A mighty change with an added dimension. Not singularly this time. Simultaneously, with Dallas. With a man.

I'd spent so much of my life in a universe where nothing made sense. It was chaotic, with everything spinning out of its orbit. The gravitational pull always seemed to be taking me in the wrong direction.

But now, chaos turned to order with a single embrace. All the planets became aligned, as if they'd been that way since the beginning. There was a visceral sense of "kingdoms, principalities, and powers, dominions, all heights and depths."[5]

Dallas spoke again with the same soft, rich, deep voice.

"I don't know how I could have helped you back then. I just wish you didn't have to go through all that. Especially not alone. I should have been there."

We cried together. Tears for me, for him, for us.

Time was transcended in a way only grace could enable. It felt as though we went back to when I was young. I had a sense that Dallas was there, comforting me. Having Dallas hold me, having a man that I trusted and loved there to provide safety and comfort when I'd been so vulnerable, it was a miraculous feeling. It was a miracle.

The mistrust I'd had for Dallas, for men in general, was swallowed up in the infinite Atonement. Past, present and future swirled about in paradisiacal glory.

Of all the many scenarios I had conjured up in my mind while camping, this was nowhere among them. Nothing in my wildest imagination had approached this.

I began to talk, only to feel interrupted by a silence that demanded an audience.

The "Lord was not in the wind … not in the earthquake … not in the fire: and after the fire a still small voice."[6]

Then we spoke gently into that good night.

At some point, we tried to eat a cold dinner. Neither one of us was very hungry.

11:49. "Oh, I lost all track of time. I should get going." Dallas stood up and pulled an envelope from his pocket.

"Here. It's only two pages, not *a hundred and forty two*. I did my best."

Almost as quickly as I'd handed him my manuscript, he gave me his letter and said goodnight.

He started to leave, and then turned back. I was still standing in the doorway.

He held me close again and then we kissed. A mutual, synchronous expression of intimacy, trust, spirituality and, what I found to be most intoxicating, unconditional love.

He knew everything there was to know about me, even the very worst of it, and loved me still. Not in spite of it all, which was the best I had hoped for, but because of it all.

I closed the door and collapsed on the couch. So much had happened, so many feelings, such intense emotions. I started to sort through it all but realized reading his letter would probably be easier.

Dallas told me he'd written the letter late Friday night, after he'd completed my manuscript. My story left him with the undeniable feeling that if I could give up so much for the Savior, certainly he could sacrifice his intellectualization of the gospel. He wanted a committed relationship with the Savior and with me. He realized that what he'd considered to be his greatest asset – his intellect – had become his greatest weakness.

If God drove into town in a '58 DeSoto, Dallas figured he knew what to say. If God came to earth in a spaceship, he knew just what to do. If God was the sum of all human hope, he knew what to think. He'd logically prepared himself for whatever the universe might send his way.

However, he had not prepared himself for the God who sneaks into your heart and breaks it so that a mighty change can occur.

He said Saturday morning, after reading the manuscript and offering up his intellectualization of the gospel, he even *felt* different. He went down to unlock his bike so he could ride to the beach, just like he had done every other Saturday morning. Try as he might, he couldn't remember the combination. He had unlocked it so many times before, without the slightest hesitation. Yet, that morning, he couldn't recall the sequence of numbers, no matter how hard he tried.

Dallas had gone from his head to his heart, overnight.

Although he wasn't aware of it at the time, it became obvious that he had experienced the mighty change. It was for Dallas as it was for the Lamanites who "were baptized with fire and with the Holy Ghost, and they knew it not."[7] The culmination of it had taken place in two days, similar to what occurred with people like Alma, King Lamoni and the queen, the father of King Lamoni and his entire household.

I'd always been jealous of the people in the scriptures for whom the mighty change occurred within hours or days.

Mine took years. I figured it didn't happen so quickly or dramatically in our day. But I was privileged to witness an equally fast and powerful mighty change with Dallas.

He had begun turning toward the Lord months earlier. However, the vast majority of his change occurred over the weekend, after he gave up all his sins to know God.

That explained why he looked different, why his countenance had changed. And, in part, that was why I'd gone from not wanting to be physical with him to feeling like we would be together through time and all eternity.

In the letter, Dallas wrote:

"My hobby has been to take apart the machines that breathe life into you, as an intellectual exercise, if I can be accused of possessing intellect, and to then leave the parts strewn about the workshop.

"The essential goodness of your words swept away all before me, laying bare something wonderful. All my best ideas, built on what I considered a firm ground of examination and rational thought, built to answer a deep hunger for understanding, built to withstand the occasional falling elephant, were reduced to scrap by the butterfly.

"I'd been convicted by your words. If you could sacrifice so much and endure such pain, certainly I could set aside my deconstruction of what we both know to be true.

"I have only heard of such sorrows in impersonal settings, stripped of the wounding edges that friendship or intimacy bring. I cannot imagine surviving such experiences, much less thriving. I was aghast. That such things happened and I had not known nor moved swiftly to protect; that I may not be mature enough to create a proper environment in a relationship with you; and that my behavior should stand and accuse me so. I remembered those whom I had shunned for not showing strength of character, not realizing that my compassion might have been a force majeure. I recalled witty barbs, tastefully spoken in clever asides among friends that I cannot remove without injuring myself.

"Now, more than ever, I find myself wanting to participate in that 'rhubarb pie thing' and would consider myself lucky for even a crumb. Your words changed my perspective radically. More than ever, a relationship is what I want. The cause of wanting is much larger now. I must be a pig, as the society of a magical personality is evidently not enough now. I will do anything good and lay aside any burden to participate in it, if you will allow."

I was stunned by his words. I'd felt so many emotions when we were together that night, so many different emotions that I could not extract a single identifiable impression or idea.

But there, after sitting alone reading his letter at the kitchen table by the light of a small brass chandelier with only two working bulbs, a single impression came into my heart and mind, so strongly that I said it aloud:

"I am going to marry this man!"

I could hardly believe my own words. But shortly after they left my lips, I recognized them as Truth.

Nothing logical, sensible, or easy to explain – just what I'd come to expect from the Lord.

Then I remembered I'd promised to call Julie and report on the evening, no matter how late. I called her up:

"Hello."

"Julie?"

"Hey, how'd it go?"

"I'm going to marry him."

"What? You're kidding, right?"

"No, I don't think I'm kidding."

"You weren't even sure you wanted him to show up!"

"I know. I guess the Lord works in mysterious ways."

"I think *you* work in mysterious ways."

"Well, consider yourself told. We can talk more tomorrow. It's past both our bedtimes, so goodnight."

I went to bed but couldn't sleep. My whole life had just changed. Changed with Dallas, changed between us, changed between the Lord and us. And, of course, it had changed with me.

I tossed and turned my way into the wee hours of the morning. I could not rid myself of the seemingly ridiculous impression, no matter how many times I tried to chip away at it with doubt or common sense. I got on my knees several times to make sure God was truly behind it. He did not leave me hanging. Every time I knelt to pray, I felt that Dallas and I really were going to marry.

The fact that I found such reassurance in the message seemed bizarre, too.

Stranger still, I could not imagine my life proceeding any other way.

Vena amoris, the vein of love.

The following month, Dallas and I attended a family get-together in Arizona. We went for a walk late at night in the crisp desert air. The stars were brilliant, creating a thick canopy of glittering orbs, with no city lights to diminish the view.

Dallas pointed heavenward and then asked me, "Do you think that maybe you and I could create one of those some-day, together?"

I knew that was his idea of a marriage proposal. I was growing accustomed to the language of this brilliant and mysterious man who used an uncommon vernacular that ranged from "the 'r' thing" to "force majeure."

"I'd consider it a privilege and a blessing."

My response came from a place of deep conviction.

I gratefully accepted his proposal, there in the still of the night under a canopy of celestial constellations – Alpha and Omega, the Beginning and the End.

I was especially moved by his reference to the journal entry he'd read in my manuscript. The one that described the time the moon seemed so real, I felt I could reach up and start molding it. When I received the impression, "You will do this someday."

The contrast was striking. Thinking back to that night I'd written the journal entry about the moon in the thick of the battle, compared to that night in the Arizona desert where I accepted Dallas' marriage proposal – without reser-vation and with blissful anticipation.

Sure, other women might prefer a fancy dinner and a formal proposal on bended knee with the presentation of a diamond-laden ring.

Not I.

To this day, I wear a simple gold band Dallas placed on the fourth finger of my left hand after we were sealed in the temple. He wears a similar ring on his left fourth finger.

The tradition of the wedding ring being placed on the fourth finger of the left hand began back when people thought that finger contained a vein that ran directly to the heart. The Latin term *vena amoris* literally means "vein of love." And v*ena amoris* fits perfectly into Dallas' special language.

We went to Dallas' home in Utah for Thanksgiving so I could meet his family. I was nervous, but it couldn't have gone better. His parents were kind and gracious. The whole family was so welcoming. It was like I was a hero. They were so grateful that this 37-year-old bachelor was actually engaged *and* active in the church again *and* getting married in the temple.

What a great way to join a new family.

I even felt like they might be accepting of my past and the book I'd written. Of course, I decided to wait to test that theory.

A proper sendoff.

As a wedding gift, Carlfred Broderick gave us a premarital couple's counseling session. He listed five things that he felt were important for Dallas and I to remember:

1. With regard to our relationship, it's important to take our shoes off because we're walking on sacred ground. Be kind and gentle with each other's hearts.

2. Whatever we look for, we'll find. If we look for

the good in each other and our relationship, we'll find it. If we look for the bad, we'll find that instead. He recommended the good.

3. Put our spouse's needs ahead of our own as often as possible. Selflessness is important for devoted spouses as well as devoted disciples.

4. Getting along is far more important than being right. (Sure, I could give up women, but give up wanting to be right?)

5. Neither one of us can remember the fifth one, which has bugged me over the years.

Priesthood powers.

Dallas and I discussed eloping to Hawaii, just the two of us, where we could be sealed in the temple on the island of Oahu. Under the radar and under the watchful care of heaven. We realized there probably wasn't a lot of eloping going on in temples. We loved the idea though.

However, Dallas' father was a temple sealer. We didn't want to miss out on the privilege of being sealed by him. Dallas had received every other priesthood ordinance from his father.

His dad's priesthood lineage could be traced back from Moroni Lundberg to William Horsley to Charles Kelly to Lorenzo Snow. From Lorenzo Snow it goes back to Heber C. Kimball then Oliver Cowdery to Peter, James and John, and then, of course, to Jesus Christ.

I've always been in awe of priesthood lineage, that the Savior physically laid his hands upon the heads of Peter, James and John, who then laid their hands upon the heads of Joseph Smith and Oliver Cowdery, who then laid their hands upon another and another and so on until Dallas' father laid his hands on Dallas' head to perform the various priesthood ordinations and blessings. That has been such a testimony to me of the significance and sacredness of the physical priesthood ordinances here on earth, as well as the powers of heaven contained therein.

We decided that if we had his parents at our wedding, we should invite mine, too, even though my dad couldn't attend the temple. So, we invited family and close friends.

As grateful recipients of priesthood power and ordination, Dallas and I knelt across from each other at the altar of the Las Vegas temple as Dallas' father sealed us for time and all eternity. We were promised that we might "inherit thrones, kingdoms, principalities, and powers" and "pass by the angels, and the gods, which are set there, to their exaltation and glory in all things."[8]

Our sealing was not only of this world. It took place as much in heaven as it did on earth.

With a great deal of effort, and with the Savior performing the greatest work of all, Dallas and I had become worthy of temple blessings and the sealing ordinance. We were able to obey the highest laws of the gospel, where "a man marry a wife by my word, which is my law, and by the new and everlasting covenant" which shall "be of full force when they are out of the world… Then shall they be gods" for "except ye abide my law ye cannot attain to this glory."[9]

A tall order, to be sure. But we had both made sacrifices and were determined to settle for nothing less.

We are still thusly determined, to this day.

After the sealing, we had a small luncheon with those who had been at the temple. Our idea of the perfect reception was no reception at all. Very little planning, no pomp or even circumstance. I was married in my white temple dress and the robes of the holy priesthood.

Rather than a formal line, we passed around our own version of a wedding album that Dallas and I had prepared beforehand. We'd put a Barbie in a wedding dress and used other Barbie dolls as bridesmaids to fill out the reception line. We had a blast picking out the wedding dress and bridesmaid dresses at Toys "R" Us. We also bought two Ken dolls, one for the groom and the other as the best man, along with two matching tuxedos.

Then we put our reception line in a bag and hauled it over to the cultural hall at the church. We set the dolls up in all the typical reception line poses and took photos. There was also red punch, butter mints and cashews in little cups. We used a Suzy Q for a wedding cake—which ended up stuck on Ken's head while we were photographing the scene in which the bride and groom stuff cake in each other's mouths.

After the film was developed, we carefully arranged all the photos in a wedding album.

Neither one of us wanted all the hassle of a big wedding, nor the tension and stress that can come with it. We wanted our wedding preparations to focus on the temple sealing and our lives together. That seemed like plenty. After all, my relationships with men had been shaky at best and Dallas had been a bachelor for almost 38 years. Not to mention, both of our relationships with the Lord had seen rough times.

In spite of our past lives, Dallas reassured us both with a simple, yet profound suggestion: "What do you say we leave all of our old baggage at the train station and just ride off together." So we did.

After the luncheon, we drove off for our honeymoon. We checked into the hotel, and Dallas carried me across the threshold into our room. Then he gently set me down on the bed and asked if I wanted a blessing.

We talked for a bit, and then he laid his hands upon my head using the same priesthood power his father had bestowed upon him and used to seal us for time and all eternity. Dallas thinned the veil as we shared a very sacred spiritual intimacy. It was a marvelous way to become of "one heart" before we became "one flesh."

I'd been so nervous about how the sexual aspect of our relationship would go. I was surprised to discover just how much it seemed to be an extension of the intimacy Dallas and I already shared.

I felt safe enough to be vulnerable, trusting enough to give my all to him. It was a complete union of bodies and souls. And miracles.

MIGHTY CHANGE IV

More mighty miracles occurred when I entered into motherhood. Growing up, I never really wanted to be a mother. As I got older, I decided that I simply lacked the mothering gene.

Mom used to say my dolls died of neglect. I knew better. I knew they had no life in them long before they came to our house. That was the problem. I wanted action and adventure, not fake tea parties with listless objects.

The only doll that really sparked my interest was Baby First Step, one of Mattel's very first battery-operated dolls. In the commercial, she went skating across the screen like Peggy Fleming on wheels. In real life, she was not nearly as impressive. Her plastic shoes were a permanent part of her feet and her socks were sewed onto her plastic skin. She had red plastic skates that went on over her shoefeet.

Thanks to the modern miracle of battery automation, her short, stiff legs could move back and forth, ever so slightly and clumsily, enabling her to walk or even roller skate – if you used a fair amount of imagination.

I'm sure my lack of interest in dolls was related to my lack of interest in live babies, too. I was the youngest child and never had to worry about caring for younger siblings. I only babysat once, when I was 13, and it was the longest three hours of my young life.

I babysat an 18-month-old toddler who started crying as soon as his parents left. Then he kept crying. And crying. I tried everything I could think of to soothe him. I held him. I set him down. I put him in the swing. I put him in his crib. I held him again. I set him down again. I tried feeding him. I tried changing his diaper. I tried every single toy I could find. Then I tried things that weren't even supposed to be toys: spatulas turned drumsticks, paper sacks, sock puppets, peek-a-boo from behind whatever, my thumb and finger with red lipstick drawn on as lips so I could finger synch the 45rpm of "Hi Ho, Hi Ho" that I played on the Close 'N Play.

After two hours of solid crying and futile attempts to soothe him, he began to vomit Lake Eerie. It was the most vomit I'd ever seen projected from a single person. And with such force! It went all over him, all over me, all over his blanket, and all over the place.

Then it was my turn to cry. Holding a vomit-covered screaming child in one arm, and a vomit-covered phone in the other, I called my mom to come and rescue us. Mostly, to rescue me. Thankfully, she came right over and helped me clean up the mess while the toddler finally collapsed and fell asleep from sheer exhaustion.

When the boy's parents returned home, they apologized and gave me a tip for my trouble. Back then, the going rate for babysitters was 50¢ an hour. So I got $1.50 regular pay, with a 75¢ bonus.

I remember thinking, "All that for 50¢ an hour? I am

never going to babysit again!"

I was good to my word.

My friends would see babies and say to the mother, "Oh, how cute! Can I hold her?" I avoided babies like the plague, especially newborns. Their heads were so heavy and wobbly. I was afraid I'd hold one and her big, heavy head would flop back and then her tiny, thin neck would break. I could just imagine handing the lifeless baby back to the mother and saying, "Gee, I am so sorry. I was careful, honest. But her head was so big and her neck was so tiny."

I assumed that the desire to mother children, and the lack thereof, was a result of the complex interplay between nature and nurture. My X and Y chromosomes indicated I was born a woman and, thusly, designed to bear children. And as I learned after I became pregnant, I was also physiologically able. Apparently my reproductive system was in proper working order. It was my emotions and my desires that had always seemed infertile.

Just because a woman is physically capable of bearing children, that doesn't mean she can mother them. The gift of mothering does not require the physical bearing of children, or even the legal adoption of them. Mother Theresa is one of the finest examples of that.

The gift and desire to mother children is irreplaceable in its potential for good and can be offered by so many different women in so many different circumstances. Friends, neighbors, extended family members, even women who are no relation whatsoever to the child. All fulfill the important and sacred duties of motherhood.

And then there's me.

Not wanting to be a mother is another desire, or lack thereof, that changed after Dallas entered my life. I began thinking of us as partners in parenthood. Dallas was kind and helpful, so I felt confident that I wouldn't have to raise kids mostly by myself. That helped take the pressure off. I thought of it in terms of parenting, not simply mothering. I began to feel more comfortable with the whole idea, and then I began to embrace it.

Expecting, but expecting what?

Before we had our first child, we thought about having Dallas quit his job to stay home with the kids because my career as an advertising copywriter was more lucrative. So, I don't think it was just coincidence that President Hinckley, as the prophet of God, first read the Family: A Proclamation to the World at the same time our first baby was born.

The proclamation states that fathers "are responsible to provide the necessities of life and protection for their families. Mothers are primarily responsible for the nurture of their children. In these sacred responsibilities, fathers and mothers are obligated to help one another as equal partners. Disability, death, or other circumstances may necessitate individual adaptation."[1]

We knew the fact that I earned more money than Dallas did not necessitate "individual adaptation." Counsel can be difficult to follow when the natural mind begs to differ. It's so much easier to have faith in our own intellect. And in the largest paycheck. However, Dallas and I had already learned that there is great wisdom in following the First Presidency, even when our intellect and feelings dictate otherwise.

We decided that Dallas should keep his full-time job and I would quit working altogether, for a time. Then I could take on a few freelance projects as time allowed.

My good friend, Dana, got married several months after I did. Talk about fertile emotional ground for mothering. Because Dana came from a family of 11 kids and was the oldest girl, she was also the mom's assistant. Mothering had always been one of her greatest gifts and strongest desires. So, the fact that she had to remain single into her 30s was difficult for her, especially because of her desire to be a mother.

We both became pregnant at about the same time. While I carried a healthy baby to full term, Dana miscarried. Eventually, she was able to bear one child and that was it. She and her husband later adopted another.

The greater trial for me was probably to be fertile and so well able to bear children. The greater trial for Dana was to be infertile and unable to bear children. More evidence that God's ways truly are not ours.

I got pregnant one year into our marriage. In fact, on our first anniversary, I woke up with morning sickness for the first time. We'd planned a day hike, which ended up being a half-hour hike. I felt so sick to my stomach, especially because I had to eat my words. I'd always had a high pain tolerance and seldom got sick, so I figured morning sickness would be no big deal. Boy was I wrong.

Because I was 35 years old, they considered mine to be an advanced-age pregnancy, which fell into the "high-risk" category. At my very first doctor visit, I trustingly thought we'd discuss what to expect during this wondrous stage of life. Instead, the geneticist (I was "so old" they immediately assigned me a geneticist) went on and on about the odds of having a baby with Down syndrome or any number of additional anomalies, along with the insistence that I should have an amniocentesis.

I immediately said no. The doctor insisted, and refused to take no for an answer. He continued to warn me about all the things that could go wrong and why I was irresponsible because I was refusing an amnio. He seemed to take offense that I would not heed his expert, professional advice.

I said no again, thanked him for his time, and rushed out of his office.

Hello and welcome to motherhood!

My morning sickness quickly turned to morning, noon and night sickness. As I began to show, comments poured in from everywhere. Even total strangers would approach me, touch my stomach (yes, *my* stomach), and talk about matters I didn't even want to discuss with close friends. The sudden loss of boundaries was unnerving.

Once I was in line at the grocery store and the woman ahead of me looked at my stomach and then she said, quite loudly, "How exciting. How far along are you?"

"Seven months."

"Oh, I had the worst hemorrhoids at seven months. Do you have hemorrhoids?"

I looked at her, and then at the rest of the people in line who seemed to be waiting for my answer. I was just grateful I didn't have any Preparation H in my shopping cart.

"Uhhh, no. I haven't had any problems with that. I guess I'm just lucky."

"Oh, you betcha. Believe me, honey." She wished me well

as she grabbed her grocery bags and walked away.

Sure, I was expecting. But what I was expecting was not at all what I got.

"Fathers and mothers are obligated to help one another as equal partners."

Dallas and I entered parenthood in much the same way that we entered marriage. We were prayerful and received the confirmation it was right. Then we pressed forward with faith in every footstep–our footsteps, followed by the tiny ink footprints on the birth certificate of our little 7-pound, 11-ounce miracle.

Marie arrived with heaven still dripping from her feet. We felt like our home was some sort of way station between heaven and earth. The knowledge that together Dallas and I had created life–with heaven largely responsible–drew us together in a whole new way.

The first two weeks after her birth were unlike any other earthly experience. I stood in awe as I held her precious little body against mine, with her soft, fuzzy head on my shoulder. I could hardly take it all in.

Marie slept quite a bit, at first. When she was awake, she was calm and content. Occasionally, she'd let out a little coo that had to be the sound young angels make when they're too content for words.

As I'd tuck my nose into the soft hair of her head, the heavenly scent created another of those experiences that took me back, or forward, to a place that was distantly and powerfully familiar. Like I was home, where it seemed as if I had always been a mother.

The spirit of that sacred calling took hold with divine swiftness and majesty. I cannot take credit for it, except to say that I had done everything I could in order to get myself to that point.

It is by grace that I was transformed into a mother in a glorious, miraculous way.

Of course, as life would have it, basking in the light of peaceful motherhood only lasted for two weeks. Then, right at day 15, someone pulled the plug. Our happy, glorious gift from heaven was replaced with a screaming, discontented foghorn in the flesh.

Thankfully, my mother came out to help. Then Dallas' mom came out to help. We tried everything we could think of to stop Marie from crying. Nothing seemed to help.

I held her. I set her down. I put her in the swing. I put her in her crib. I held her again. I set her down again. I put warmer clothes on her. I put cooler clothes on her. I tried feeding her. I tried changing her diaper.

Unfortunately, no amount of Mattel's battery-operated technology could have prepared me for this.

After exhausting nearly every possibility, time and time again, Dallas and I happened upon a winner–if discovering such a laborious technique could be considered winning. We found that if we bounced Marie about six inches away from the body, at a 45-degree angle, at the rate of approximately 100 bounces per minute while making a "shushing" sound, she'd calm down and quit crying.

If we changed the angle or the rate, she'd start crying again. As long as we kept her in constant motion, she was content. And I do mean constant motion.

The swing would work for a short time. Walking her in the stroller or in a front pack would work for a while. Driving her around in the car would work for a while. And then there was the bouncing.

All day long, I'd alternate between them. Then when Dallas got home from work, I'd pass her off to him, like a football, just as I collapsed in a heap.

I learned the polite, quasi-technical catchall diagnosis for this condition on my next trip to the pediatrician.

"Well, your baby looks perfectly healthy. She's in the 75th percentile for weight and 89th percentile for length."

"But she cries all the time, unless we bounce her."

"Then she must be colicky."

"Everyone says she must be colicky. But what does that mean, exactly?"

"It's when an otherwise healthy baby cries an inordinate amount of time."

"Yes, but what causes it?"

"We aren't sure. It could be gastrointestinal, or maybe neurological."

"The stomach or the brain? I've read about it, but what can we do to help her?"

"We don't really know that, either. Some babies are just fussy. It should go away at 3 or 4 months."

Some babies are just fussy? Marie was beyond the 99th percentile of fussiness. So there I was, a new mother who had little experience with typical babies, raising a "colicky" one that not even the experts knew how to help.

Our bouncing baby girl continued to bounce, thanks to

the never-ending work of Dallas and me.

At three months, she was still colicky. That's also when she quit napping altogether, unless I drove her around in the car. She'd sleep for about 45 minutes as long as I kept driving. She'd wake up the moment I turned off the car, sometimes even when I stopped at a stoplight. So, I began taking her for daily afternoon drives on the freeway where I didn't have to stop at stoplights.

Plenty of people had plenty of advice.

"Just set her down and let her cry it out."

"Put her in a playpen."

"Hold her as she cries. She'll learn to stop eventually."

"Maybe she has an upset stomach. Give her gripe water." (That was properly named, to be sure.)

"Don't wrap her too tightly."

"Maybe she needs more stimulation."

"Maybe she's too stimulated."

Admittedly, we tried everything anybody suggested. But alas, it was to no avail.

When Marie was six months old, Dallas and I decided to attend the temple together for the first time since her birth. Yes, our once-a-week temple attendance had come to a screeching, crying halt. We hadn't used a sitter very much because Marie would cry the whole time. I didn't have the heart to put Marie or the babysitter through that (although we did pay more that 50¢ an hour).

I asked a friend of mine to watch her while we attended a temple session because she lived near the L.A. Temple. By the time we returned from our session, Marie had just barely fallen asleep but was still making those little post-sobbing noises. Her hair and shirt were soaking wet from her tears.

My friend apologized profusely. "I'm so sorry. I tried the bouncing thing. Then I tried everything I could think of but she just kept crying the whole time you were gone. Finally, she got so exhausted, she fell asleep."

So much for our temple attendance together as a couple. We started taking turns going to the temple, on occasion.

The daily grind became more and more grinding. Dallas would come home tired from work and hope to rest. But I'd spent the day bouncing and swinging and taking care of Marie, with a midday drive for her nap being the closest thing to a break I could get.

Whenever Dallas got home late from work, I'd get upset because it seemed like all I could do was make it until 6:00. That was my mark for the day. I'd watch the clock as 6:00 approached. Each second ticked by slowly with an onerous tick tick tick tick tick.

I finally had my sister come out and take care of Marie for a few nights so we could get her to sleep through the night instead of waking up every two hours. That worked to some degree. Instead of every two hours, she'd go four hours before waking and crying.

I'm sure they use sleep deprivation as a form of torture somewhere. It was certainly torture for Dallas and me.

In the "Cry Research Letter," we actually found some helpful information about colic. "Crying and the fatigue that typically accompanies it can inflict enormous emotional strain causing parents to feel they are providing inadequate care, triggering anxiety, stress, resentment and low self-esteem."[2]

There were many times I felt inadequate, like my lack of mothering skills was the root cause of the problem. When anxiety and stress took over, it became more difficult to think clearly and receive inspiration.

Fortunately, there were times that I prayed and felt I was doing all I could and that heaven was pleased. If only I could have kept that truth in mind more often. But, the lack of sleep and pure exhaustion were clouding my mind.

By the time Marie turned one, I begged Dallas to quit his job and find a way to work from home. I was working part time from home, mostly late at night, and it looked like we could make it financially if I worked a little more while he helped with Marie.

Dallas could tell I had reached a breaking point, so he agreed to quit work and start a business with a friend. That was such a huge blessing for me–physically, emotionally, and spiritually.

Another benefit of having Dallas share so much in the caretaking, 50/50, sometimes more, was that it enabled him to understand just how much work it can be to raise children. Even one child.

I don't think anyone can understand how much work it is to care for children unless they're responsible for them a large part of the day, every day, for months. It helped our relationship so much to have Dallas understand. Unfortunately, that made life harder for him.

More sacrifices bring forth more blessings.

I knew motherhood would be challenging, especially since I'd watched what my sister went through with her three kids. Two of them had special challenges. Nonetheless, I had no idea just how hard, or rewarding, it could be.

Sometimes I'd take on freelance projects at an ad agency that involved working there several days, all day long. And I swear, give me 14-hour workdays at an office anytime. At least I'd get a lunch hour with people my age, during which I could eat food that someone else had prepared and I didn't have to feed to anybody else. My co-workers were perfectly capable of feeding themselves. They also provided interesting adult conversation.

Dallas and I both sacrificed full-time salaries, alone time, most of our time spent together as a couple, frequent temple attendance, even a good night's sleep. No doubt all of those sacrifices that we made for Marie helped us to become so very attached to her, and to the children that would follow.

We would do anything, give up everything, go to the end of the universe and back for our children. I've come to comprehend, in a more personal and celestial way, the love that our Heavenly Parents have for us, thanks to the blessing of having our own children.

From the first day a new little soul arrived in our home, during those first two weeks of pure parental peace and joy, and throughout the torturous schedule that fell upon us with a reverberating and repeating thud, I was given the power to not only endure but also attend with a divine sense of motherly duty and love – far beyond that which I would have been capable of if left to my own devices.

Sure, there was probably some remote mothering gene hidden deep within my DNA that sprang into action and expressed itself when triggered by pregnancy. Every fiber of my being no doubt took part in those major physiological changes.

Yet, there was always something more. It was obvious, on so many occasions, that our Heavenly Parents were guiding us and the Savior was continually transforming our lives.

Looking back at how exhausting it all was, and how it pushed me to the very edge, I would change very little. One thing I *would* change is that I'd have much more confidence in how we felt we should handle our children and less confidence in how others thought we should handle them.

For a time, I mistakenly thought that since motherhood didn't seem to come naturally to me, then the other mothers must know far more than I. They were certainly helpful, in many ways. But when it came right down to it, Dallas and I were the only two people who actually held the mantle of parenthood for our unique children—as well as our Heavenly Parents, of course.

Eventually, I found confidence in knowing that heaven put Dallas and me in charge. He knew just how imperfect we would be, and in what ways our imperfections would manifest themselves. Sometimes my lack of native skills was a positive thing because it caused me to seek divine guidance that much more often.

Plus, it was my divine nature, not my earthly nature, which served to bring about the mighty change that enabled me to become a true mother, rather than simply a woman biologically capable of bearing children.

Like mother, not always like daughter.

Talk about a complex, unpredictable interplay of nature

and nurture. When Marie turned two, she became a lover of dolls and all things satin and lace. She grew like a dainty little flower and loved to flit about the house dressed up in three or four layers of fancy dress-up clothes. Her favorite doll was also her favorite story: Madeline.

I grew to love the Madeline books, too. I'm sure part of my attraction to them was that I related so well to poor Miss Clavel. She was always busy trying to keep track of 12 little girls and put them in 2 straights lines, with the smallest one who was Madeline.

I figured the conversion rate was pretty close. My 1 to Miss Clavel's 12. I'd been so uninclined to be a caretaker, and Miss Clavel so superinclined. Otherwise, why would she work at a boarding school caring for 12 little girls? And in my frequent isolation from almost all adults, Miss Clavel would be the one woman to whom I could relate.

"And afraid of a disaster, Miss Clavel ran fast and faster."[3]

The slightest noise would send me running to Marie's room to check on her. Even the lack of noise would send me running. Was she still breathing? Was she all right?

My dad came out one week to help me and my husband build a rather large playhouse, complete with small loft, winding staircase, double-paned windows, electrical outlets, and an Astroturf covered porch with a little white picket fence. Marie and I held many a tea party in there. I even managed to be the perfect co-hostess, treating her listless, lifeless dolls with newfound respect as the living, breathing beings Marie was certain they were.

I spoke with the utmost dignity as I picked up the teapot

filled with tea (chocolate milk). "Oh, welcome to our humble abode Miss Madeline. We're so happy to have you. May I get you some delicious tea and crumpets?"

Then I'd pour some for Miss Snuffles, too, the beloved sheep that never missed a single tea party. After serving our guests first, I'd pour some for Marie and me. Then I'd pick up the teacup and sip, with my pinkie perfectly poised.

Now, if that isn't a testament to the power of the mighty change, I don't know what is.

Increasing exponentially.

Despite our fears that a second child might be as fussy as the first, we wanted Marie to have a sibling. Again, I was able to get pregnant rather quickly.

Having a two-year-old running around while I was experiencing morning sickness and all the other bodily changes was difficult, for sure. Most of that pregnancy is foggy. Not remembering it is a blessing, I'm sure. Or, just the natural result of self-preservation.

What I remember most is the time I was lying there on the couch feeling so sick and so exhausted, I couldn't move. I heard Marie in the kitchen, digging through the drawers. We had a knife drawer, which was forbidden, making it that much more intriguing, of course. And she had learned how to work the drawer child guards, more quickly than Dallas and I had learned, of course.

I yelled to her in the kitchen, "Marie, you be sure and stay out of that knife drawer."

"Yes, Mom."

Such two-year-old compliance made me suspicious. I

knew I should get up and go see whether or not she was in the knife drawer. But I felt so sick, I simply could not move. So, I said a short prayer. "Heavenly Father, please don't let Marie hurt herself with a knife. Amen." That took all the energy I could muster.

I continued to listen carefully, in case there was a scream or she dropped to the floor. I kept wondering why on earth I thought my first pregnancy was so hard when I didn't have any other kids to worry about. I was amazed at how the difficulty of motherhood increased exponentially while the number of children increased with simple addition. In fact, there weren't even two children in the home yet and I was already wondering whether or not I'd live through it all.

I'd always been quite adept at completing tasks, performing well at my job, and showing a fair amount of talent in a few areas. But child bearing and rearing? Oh my!

Why on earth didn't someone tell me motherhood could be traumatic at times? It must be some sort of Darwinian thing. The preservation of the species. Some secret code of silence.

"Don't spread the word about the challenges of motherhood or we'll become extinct."

By the grace of God, Ann was born healthy and proved to be no fussier than the typical baby. Marie was absolutely thrilled to have another "doll" to play with.

After Ann turned eighteen months, it was obvious she was every bit as much the satin, lace and dolls, sugar and spice and everything nice kind of girl as her older sister. And instead of having tea parties where Ann replaced Miss Madeline or Miss Snuffles, everyone stayed and we had to make room for Ann's little friend, Molly.

Now, Molly was, quite honestly, the most pathetic doll you'd ever want to meet. She'd get dragged from place to place, sandbox to swing to tea party to bed and back around again. If you were looking for Ann, you could just follow the trail of threads and stuffing left behind by raggedy Molly.

I began plotting ways in which we might be able to put poor Molly out of her misery without Ann having a meltdown. Nothing ever worked. She was far too attached, and I just didn't have the heart.

It didn't take long for Ann to reach the point where she put away childish things and went for modern technology instead. She became enamored with the ads for Amazing Amanda, the Superdoll of the Century.

Christmas was coming, the goose was getting fat, and the ads for Amazing Amanda were running thick. I considered buying the doll, until I found out that she cost over a hundred dollars.

"More than a hundred dollars for a doll? You've got to be kidding!"

In addition to being a satin and lace kind of girl, Ann is also the Great Negotiator. She is bright, stubborn, quick as a whip, and articulate well beyond her years. So, she began preparing her case that would prove, beyond a shadow of a doubt, that she needed Amazing Amanda for Christmas.

And talk about a generation gap. I'd been impressed by the doll who could shuffle her legs a bit while powered by two D batteries. Amazing Amanda was a true wonder of digital technology. She incorporated facial robotics, speech-recognition, memory chips, and radio frequency tags that resulted in the most lifelike doll ever. (Ann could tell you all this because she knew it by heart.) Amanda could ask for a certain food and recognize what it was: peas, cookies, pizza, or popcorn. She could tell you the date, the time, and wish you happy birthday, on your birthday. She'd go to sleep at night with a yawn and a goodnight, then wake up in the morning with a timely "Good morning." She could even say when she needed to go to the bathroom and came with her own potty seat.

"And she does all that for just over one hundred dollars," Ann would say, in her best advertising voice.

"Honey, I am telling you, a hundred dollars is way too much for a doll?"

"But Mom, no other doll in the world can do what Amanda does. She really is amazing!"

"Ann, you aren't listening to me. I-am-not-getting-you-Amazing-Amanda-for-Christmas! I know that she talks and asks for popcorn and eats it and poops and tells you exactly when and where she pooped. But dear, I don't care if she comes with her own jetpack and can circle the neighborhood. I am not going to spend a hundred dollars for a doll!"

"OK then. I'll ask Santa Claus."

"Santa is NOT bringing you Amazing Amanda, either. That's it. End of discussion."

I walked out of the room as fast as I could, feeling like I was losing an argument with a small child, yet again.

"And afraid of a disaster, Miss Clavel ran fast and faster."

Unfortunately, I couldn't run quite fast enough to avoid hearing Ann as I ran out of sight. "I'm writing a letter to Santa Claus right now!"

When Christmas morning rolled around, Ann made a beeline for the present from my mom, her loving and generous Nana. Ann had already examined every present under the tree, many times over. You could tell that the wrapping paper had been unwrapped and put back in place. Well, sort of back in place anyway.

And who needs Santa when you have Nana.

"Oh look," Ann said, in her sweet, innocent baby voice, which I knew was a pretend voice. Her other pretend voice was an authoritative adult voice that she sometimes used when she was negotiating. "I think I'll open this present from Nana. I wonder what she got me."

From the looks of the multi-folded wrapping paper and the barely sticking, well-worn tape, I figured she'd opened the present from Nana at least five times.

Using her fake baby voice again, only louder and more excitedly, "Oh my goodness, look! It's Amazing Amanda!"

And that was the morning Amazing Amanda joined our family. Actually, she didn't officially join our family until we programmed her to do so, which took most of Christmas day. Ann had to speak to her in order to set the appropriate voice recognition – imprinting, we'll call it.

Amanda actually did most of what the television commercials promised. (False advertising had become illegal since the time of those Baby First Steps ads that showed the doll skating around like Peggy Fleming.)

"Amanda, what would you like to eat?" Ann asked Amanda, who had her own chair at our dinner table.

"I'd like pizza, please." Ann put a plastic cookie in her mouth instead. But that Amanda, she knew better.

"That's not pizza. I'd like pizza please."

I have to say, and this is not just my dislike for dolls in general, honestly. I found Amazing Amanda to be kind of creepy. Christmas night, I walked into Ann's room and I couldn't tell whether or not she was asleep in the dark. Just in case, I said, "Goodnight Bug."

From under the covers came Amanda's muffled voice. "You don't sound like Mommy." She startled me. I couldn't help but feel like it was something out of a horror film.

I seldom knew where Amazing Amanda might be hiding. I'd say something to someone, and then from out of nowhere would come this, "You don't sound like Mommy." I swear. I wasn't even safe in my own home.

I was pleased to learn that I wasn't the only one afraid of a doll. I checked on the Internet one day and found comments like, "The Amazing Amanda doll, frankly, scares us." Also, "Amazing Amanda: cute doll or tool of Satan?" The article called her "the little possessed doll." And, no doubt my favorite, "She must be the Bride of Chucky!"

Creepy or not, the spoils had gone to Amazing Ann. Again. I don't know how or why this happens. Logic dictates that full-grown adults with average intelligence and years of life experience should be able to outmaneuver and outsmart children ranging in age from newborn to 18 years old. But that simply is not the case.

I started to blame my repeated defeats on my own lack of mothering skills. However, I began to observe the same phenomenon happening with parents and children everywhere. At the grocery store, the school, the playground, the toy store. Especially the toy store. That place is a dense minefield just waiting for exhausted parents with combat-ready children. Even the toy packaging provides ammo for the pint-sized militia.

"Look mom! It shoots water balloons over 50 feet. Hours of excitement. And no batteries necessary!"

"Daddy, can I ride it, can I ride it, can I? Just look. Two speeds, twice the fun!"

I must say, despite all of her negotiating and her creepy doll that fortunately did fall from grace, eventually, Ann truly is amazing. No batteries necessary. She'll fix me a plate of snacks and sneak it into my bedroom to surprise me. She'll tidy up an area and spruce it up with flowers, knick-knacks, photo frames, whatever she can find. And we love to lie down together on the living room floor in front of the big window and soak up the sun, like a pair of lizards on a rock.

That must be some sort of Darwinian thing, too. Despite all the trouble and effort, the young take on an irresistible charm that makes them valuable beyond measure. I'm sure that's what keeps them safe under the watchful care of loving parents – as long as the mother isn't pregnant again and passed out on the couch.

Recovering the body, restoring the soul.

They recovered the bodies of John F. Kennedy, Jr., his wife Carolyn, and her sister Lauren on July 21, 1999. They finally found the wreckage of their plane that disappeared several days before. Television stations could broadcast nothing else.

One newscaster commented that we would remember what we were doing that day, just like we remembered what we were doing the day John F. Kennedy, Sr. was shot. That seemed like a gross exaggeration. But I knew I'd remember what I was doing that day, and not because of the Kennedys.

On July 21, 1999, I donned a drafty, immodest hospital gown as I lay on a cold metal bed in a stark hospital room staring at a wall with nothing but a TV, and the Kennedys.

You'd think I could have appreciated some aspect of the alone time. I seldom, if ever, had the luxury of watching TV in the middle of the day. Whenever I tried turning the TV on, it would attract my young girls like nocturnal flying insects when you turn on the porch light. They'd interrupt even before the show's sponsors had the chance. Then, with "Mary Poppins" or "Wallace and Gromit" or "Creature Comforts" in hand, they'd pop in a video and sit down with me to watch, thinking they'd done me a favor by saving me from regular television. They were probably right.

Now, in the hospital, I felt so alone. I mean, lonely. It had been so many years since I'd felt lonely. Especially since I'd spent the past three months in the constant company of our third child in the making–24 hours a day, seven days a week–as he went from fertilized egg to embryo to fetus.

And now to miscarriage.

The doctor had done an ultrasound and decided there was no longer a growing, vibrant baby inside. Just a week after announcing that we were expecting a baby, we had to retract the statement.

I was given the option of letting everything come out naturally or having a D&C. After two days of bleeding, it felt like trauma by slow drip. So, I opted for the get-it-over-as-quickly-as-possible routine.

I held the remote control tightly, clicking it again and again as if I were tapping out an S.O.S. in Morse code. I tapped from channel to channel, desperately searching for something besides footage of dead Kennedys. I was searching for solace.

We'd seriously considered stopping with two children. We loved our two beautiful, healthy girls and they were certainly more than enough to keep us busy. Plus, Dallas and I weren't getting any younger. In fact, having two kids seemed to add years to our lives. I'm not sure how old we'd become in parent years. In regular people years, I was 40 and Dallas was 45. His hair had turned far greyer, and whiter, with each child.

Regardless, every time we tried to make the decision that we were done, we felt uncomfortable about it. So, we fasted and prayed and took it to the Lord in the temple. It was there that we both felt impressed that another member of our family was out there somewhere.

We weren't the only ones hesitant about us having a third child. When Dallas made his weekly phone call to his parents, he decided to tell them about the inspiration we received at the temple. His folks were avid temple workers.

"Dallas, can you handle another child?" His mother was genuinely concerned, not nosey. I'm sure she doesn't have a nosey bone in her body.

"Well, we fasted and prayed and took it to the Lord, in the temple." Dallas figured mentioning the temple would ease her worries. Her response surprised us both. "Why did you do that? If you ask that kind of a question in the temple, you know what the answer will be! For heaven's sake!"

My mom was concerned, too. However, the impression came strong and sure, so we moved forward, again, in faith.

After the miscarriage, I couldn't help but wonder why the impression had been so strong. We simply could have stopped at two, and I wouldn't have been lying there in the hospital waiting for the doctor to go in and recover the body of what had been our third child.

Dana, having been through it herself, said it's like your child has died but there's no funeral. No formal recognition of the loss. No procession. No flowers. Just your own writhing, cramping body with a dreadful concoction of hormones and emotions wreaking havoc.

They kept showing the Kennedys' apartment in New York. Mourners had put so many flowers in front of their place that they had to start moving them to nursing homes, hospitals, and cemeteries.

The doctor finally arrived. As they wheeled me down the hall, I stared straight up at the ceiling. A persistent squeak from one of the wheels was in syncopated rhythm with the harsh flash-flash-flash of the fluorescent lights flickering past overhead. A series of offbeat tones at varying pitches signaled the staff. Together, it created a bizarre cacophony of sight and sound, reminding me of an opening scene from an old Twilight Zone episode.

It was the longest hall I'd ever travelled down. I found myself wondering what I'd wondered so many times before. When does life really begin? Does the spirit enter the body upon conception? Could the spirit for this body-gone-awry have another chance?

Before my miscarriage, I'd only pondered such questions

from the detached podium of speculation. Now, it all took on a very personal significance.

The anesthesiologist smiled as he put a mask on me. After a few deep breaths, I was out. Next thing I knew, I was in the recovery room. As the medication wore off and the cramping increased, I was reminded of the deep emotional pain of my loss. I tried to remember back when I did not identify as a mother, had no desire to be a mother, and could have cared less whether or not I had children. But I could not call to heart those feelings or that time period. All I knew was the deep ache and sense of loss I felt because of my missing child, with two already at home.

I stayed in bed all day the following day, not so much in need of physical healing as emotional and spiritual. No doubt the hormonal mayhem added to the upheaval.

When Dallas arrived back home to find me in bed he said, "Are you still in pain?"

"Yeah. Mostly heartache." I started to cry.

"What's wrong?"

I was bothered by the fact he even had to ask. "Well, I did just have a miscarriage."

"We can try again." He had immediately gone into the "let me try to fix it" mode. That was something he could do, which is so important for so many men.

I wish I could have been grateful he was trying to help. Instead, I snapped back. "I know we can! That still doesn't change the fact that I just lost a baby! *We* just lost a baby."

"But honey, it hadn't even developed yet."

In an effort to fix things, he was only making it worse. Plus, he wasn't right. The baby had developed. For three months, I'd created a child. I'd even felt impressed he was a boy. I breathed life into him, not so much with amniotic fluid, but with hopes and dreams. I'd held him in my arms and kissed him on the nape of his neck, just below his soft hair. I'd envisioned my husband giving him a name and a blessing. I'd witnessed his baptism and priesthood ordinations. He passed the sacrament, then blessed it, then served a full-time mission.

It's amazing what the human mind can do with a mere cluster of cells.

"So then none of this should matter, right?" I shouted at Dallas in frustration.

"That's not what I meant." He continued to maintain the calm, soothing tenor of his deep voice.

"I know." I'd gone from sadness to anger to acceptance in just a few sentences.

I'd lost a baby and I had no idea where to find him.

I would experience all the stages of grief over the next few months. I kept thinking Dallas should be going through them, too. We'd celebrated the creation of a new life together. Shouldn't we mourn the loss together, too?

I expected Dallas to feel like I did. We'd been one in so many ways. But he was not the mother. He was the father. He was not the one who carried a child within. My body had already been caring for a baby. And so had my heart.

As grace would have it, I was blessed with a tender mercy that evening. The week before, we'd finally sent off a bunch of rolls of film we'd collected over the years so they could be developed. The prints arrived in the mail that day.

There were photos of so many things I'd forgotten, but

the camera remembered with clarity. Marie in the hospital, just after she was born. Ann just after she was born, with Marie sitting on the hospital bed holding her. Marie, age three, dressed in several layers of dress up clothes. The Halloween where Marie was a pumpkin and Ann was a little black cat. Dallas swinging the girls on the outdoor swing that sent them soaring over a steep hill just beyond our back fence. Even photos from our honeymoon.

Six years of memories and family and life, all spread out on the kitchen table.

A wave of love and mercy and grace washed over me. I was filled with such gratitude for what I already had. It helped buffer the loss of what I'd yet to gain.

"I will also ease the burdens which are put upon your shoulders, that even you cannot feel them upon your backs, even while you are in bondage; and this will I do that ye may stand as witnesses...that I, the Lord God, do visit my people in their afflictions."[4]

The Lord truly does visit us in our afflictions–usually in unexpected ways. I stand as witness.

Dallas helped as I healed. When I could not bring myself to fix dinner, he fixed it. When I could not bear to care for the living while I mourned for the dead, he took over. My resentment toward him for not understanding began to fade as I grew in gratitude for his protection and care. His love helped shore up my wounded heart.

Dying lessons.

Just a few days after my miscarriage, I suffered another loss Carlfred Broderick. Cancer struck its final blow on

July 27, 1999. His was a slow death. He'd begun to have stomach pain and lose weight. The initial diagnosis was an ulcer. Months passed as the pain and weight loss continued. So did the poking, prodding, and battery of tests. Along with all the misdiagnoses. Physicians eventually concluded his problem must be psychosomatic.

When the doctor recommended he see a psychotherapist, Dr. Broderick laughed and said, "Which therapist do you recommend? I have helped train most of the good ones in Southern California."

It would have been an arrogant statement coming from someone else. From Dr. Broderick, it was actually true.

After a year had gone by, he sought the advice of a specialist who made the first and last correct diagnosis. Cancer. Because it had been discovered late, it was inoperable.

Cancer is unimpressed by titles or accomplishments or the contributions an individual makes. It strikes without discretion, without warning, and often without mercy.

I was amazed that Carlfred didn't turn bitter because of the late diagnosis. He never asked "Why me?" Instead, he commented, "Why not me? I've heard so much of the pain and suffering of other people. Certainly it's my turn."

Forget that his biological father left before Carlfred was born, and his stepfather always told him he was good for nothing. That was history, he insisted. He had a wonderful wife he cherished, and eight kids who he said would have been good even if they'd been orphans.

The last time I visited him at his home, he was in pain and taking different medications that weren't really helping. He was too sick to eat much and he no longer left the house.

Death was at his door. "Other than the fact I'm dying, things are going great." He beamed that huge grin of his.

He stood 6'6" and probably weighed about 130 pounds by then. His skin sharply outlined his bones, and his pajamas flapped about as if they were hanging from a flagpole. Weak as he was, his long arms and hands still waved about in wild, animated gestures as he spoke. I got choked up when he raised one arm high while he told a story. His raised arm reminded me of a dream Carlfred told me about long before death had come calling.

He'd only had one dream in his life that he considered to be like a vision. He was hiking with a large crowd of people, all of whom were following the prophet and his counselors. Carlfred held his arm up high, above the crowd, so that his family could see his raised arm and follow him. When the prophet headed down what appeared to be a box canyon, many Church members refused to follow. They assumed it was a dead end and they'd be trapped.

Carlfred said he began to draw the same conclusion, and then thought better of it. He knew it didn't matter what he thought, only what the prophet thought. So, he kept his arm held up high, continued to follow the prophet, and told his family to follow his lead.

As it turned out, the canyon did not dead end. It turned sharply and opened up to a wide expanse with lush greenery and incredible vistas. He and his family gathered there, along with those Saints who had also followed the prophet.

"When the First Presidency has spoken, it is God who has spoken," Carlfred declared, with an air of authority and conviction that only someone of his stature could command.

It was evident that he knew the gospel was true, more than any of the other knowledge he'd gained on earth.

Throughout all of his intellectual and secular pursuits, Carlfred continued to follow the prophet, no matter what.

He had to retire earlier than he would have liked because of the cancer. At his USC retirement banquet, he was asked what person had been the most influential in his life. There he was among his colleagues, well-respected professors, psychologists and sociologists who were no doubt wondering who he'd choose. Plato? Sophocles? Jung?

Dr. Broderick answered, "Jesus Christ." Probably not the philosopher the audience had in mind.

At his funeral, there stood his wife and eight children, all active in the Church, following their husband and father to whatever magnificent vistas he was observing. I could just imagine Carlfred up there, with his arm raised high, following the prophets of long ago and of latter days. Still doing everything he could to make certain his family followed.

When I arrived back home from the funeral, I got out *Born That Way.* I wanted to re-read the recommendation that Dr. Broderick had so graciously written for the back cover of my book.

I thought about when I'd been working hard to get the final manuscript to print and was making a concerted effort to date men. I felt discouraged and couldn't help but wonder if my writing was for naught. In the middle of my despair, the fax machine rang. I watched as two handwritten pages from Carlfred rolled out of the machine. It was the endorsement that he had agreed to write, after he read my manuscript.

Carlfred had written: "*Born That Way* is a must read for everyone in the Church who is struggling with feelings of homosexuality – their own or another's … Erin Eldridge tells the story of her own difficult journey away from the spiritual chaos of homosexual relationships, over the bumpiest of roads, to a condition of worthiness and full participation in the gospel plan. Along the way, she received support and assistance from friends, priesthood leaders, and professional therapists. All of them were well-intentioned; some were actually helpful. (That's such a Carlfred comment.) But her ultimate triumph was Christ-centered, as, in my experience, true healing has to be.

"Both as a priesthood leader and as a professional therapist, it has been my privilege and challenge to help a number of individuals of both sexes along this same perilous path. Outside of the scriptures, I am aware of no more comprehensive and helpful mapping of the way that leads from the homosexual lifestyle back to the Tree of Life than can be found between the covers of this book."

I was so profoundly struck when I first read it, fresh off the fax machine. His timing was inspired. Apparently the spirit speaks through our hearts, our minds and, on occasion, our fax machines.

As I reread what he'd written after the funeral, I felt that same spirit again. My sadness for his loss turned to soulful gratitude. It wasn't like Bishop Garey dying so suddenly and violently. I was on solid ground when Carlfred passed away from cancer. And I'd had time to prepare.

Both were dear losses, to be sure. Still, I felt privileged that those two men, great in so many ways, had been such personal and powerful influences in my life at such pivotal times. Since both men were taken early, the timing needed to be precise in order for me to meet up with them and grow because of our association.

I could almost feel the rich, lush texture and pattern of the thickly woven tapestry of my life. It was obvious where the paths crisscrossed each other–over, under, and back across. "Such mighty works are wrought by his hands".[5]

"Therefore, they must needs be chastened and tried."

Several months after the miscarriage and Carlfred's death, I became pregnant again. At five months, an ultrasound determined the baby was a boy. Because I was 40 years old, I knew the odds of a perfectly healthy boy had been reduced with each tick of my biological clock. I didn't need a geneticist to give me the precise stats.

But this time, I had a nagging feeling something might be wrong. I tried to shake it off, assuming it was just doubt carried over from the miscarriage, which I should expect. Still, there was a deep foreboding that I could not squelch. Until the day Trent was born.

The biggest problem, I mean biggest, was the delivery.

"Push! Push!" The nurse insisted on coaching. My husband knew better. He'd learned from the first two deliveries that it's best just to keep quiet.

I have to confess, I'm not a very good Christian during childbirth.

"C'mon, push! Push harder!"

"I am pushing harder!" I roared, with the ferociousness of a bear with its foot caught in a large metal trap. It felt like that, too, only the trap was further up my body.

When all ten and a half pounds of Trent finally emerged, the doctor held him up and said, "Oh, wow. No wonder he wouldn't come out. He's huge! You really were pushing."

As the nurse was cleaning him off I kept saying, "Is he healthy? Is he healthy? Is there anything wrong with him?"

"He's fine. He's wonderful."

An oversized newborn garnered little sympathy from Dallas' side of the family. When Dallas was born, he weighed 11 pounds, 4 ounces. There was no blessed epidural, either. And that was back when doctors thought women shouldn't gain more than ten pounds with the entire pregnancy, and back when most doctors were men. Dallas' mom only gained 12 pounds with Dallas' brother, who weighed 11 pounds 6 ounces at birth. Add another couple of pounds for the placenta, and his mom actually lost weight during pregnancy. That can't be a good thing.

We named our boy Trent Carmi Campbell. Carmi was Dallas' father's name. He'd always been such a kind and gentle bearer of the priesthood, and a deeply caring father. His life was a strong and lasting example for Dallas. Our family is forever grateful that Carmi's gentle, steady influence has spanned the generations.

As we feared, three children were exponentially more challenging. As Dallas said, "We've gone from man-to-man defense to a zone defense. And the zone is bigger than two people can cover."

That pretty well summed it up.

It helped that even as a baby, Trent was happy and outgoing. Beautiful, too, with bright shining eyes that were glorious windows to his soul.

He learned to talk at a year, saying "dada" and "mama" and "bye." He also liked to make animal sounds. "What does the coyote say?" He could howl like a coyote, quack like a duck, and meow like a kitten, sort of.

However, by the time Trent reached 18 months, things began to change. Our happy, outgoing boy became fussy and withdrawn. His list of words began to decrease instead of grow. He kept biting my elbow, as if he were in pain.

I took him to the doctor who insisted he was perfectly fine. But I knew he wasn't. He quit responding to his sisters, then to his dad, and then to me. He even quit responding to his name.

Finally, he quit responding to everything, except for Veggie Tales. He'd watch Bob and Larry and friends for hours, fixated on the dancing cucumber and tomato, doing a little dance himself. He would spin in circles, on his toes, whenever the Veggie Tales Theme Song started up. (We often expressed gratitude it was Veggie Tales, though, and not Barney or Teletubbies. It was proof that we're never given more than we can bear.)

Soon, it seemed like Trent had packed up all his belongings, including his Veggie Tales pals, and moved away to his own little world, not taking a single living soul with him.

One Sunday at church, we sat behind a family who had a son with autism. They were wrestling with him and trying to get him to sit still. He kept climbing all over the pew and ignoring both parents who were visibly exasperated but amazingly patient. So I sat there watching those parents struggle with him and thought to myself, "Wow, I'm sure glad that's not me. I have a tough enough time with three typical kids. I could never do that."

Without intending to, I thought it again. "I could never do that. I could never do that."

Then, panic struck as the words took a wretched form. "I could never do that, honestly! Heavenly Father, please, there is no way I could ever handle that!"

In no time, my stream of consciousness turned to a flash flood. I knew what Trent's problem was. He was autistic.

For the rest of the day, I tried to dismiss the impression. No doubt it was simply paranoia, leftover hormones, feelings of inadequacy as a mother, or just dumb luck that we sat behind the child with autism.

There are a million ways to pass inspiration off as something more earthly, and easier to deal with.

My sister called me that evening. "You know, Danny and I were talking. I'm not trying to intrude, but we were wondering if you've ever read much about autism. I looked it up on the Internet and I think Trent might have some of the symptoms. Maybe you should check it out."

I started to cry.

"What? I'm sorry! I'm not saying he *is* autistic. I just mean maybe you should look into it."

As my body heaved from heart to toe, I confessed. "I've been feeling that maybe he is autistic. Your phone call just confirmed it."

I hung up, slowly approached the computer as if it were a bomb, and then entered the word "autism" into the search window. That was the start of my education on a subject about which I knew very little and could now write a book.

"The onset of autism that occurs between 18 months to 2 years old is called regressive autism. The child may start talking and then stop. He may spin around in circles or perform other repetitive behaviors. He might cease to respond to his name."

The more I read, the larger the pit in my stomach grew.

The following day, I called for an appointment at the children's clinic. They happened to have a cancellation the following day.

The social worker asked questions and I could tell she was focusing on autism. She asked questions similar to those I'd read on the Internet. Then she said, "I would like to have Trent back for a hearing test and an autism evaluation."

This time I didn't cry. A dry, frozen wasteland of numbness quickly settled in and spread out. I got into the car, started to drive, and quickly realized I was in no shape to operate heavy machinery or navigate through traffic.

I pulled over in an alleyway at some industrial park. I still remember staring down at the asphalt as I called Dallas to tell him what had happened. He kept reassuring me we didn't know anything for certain as I kept insisting that I did know. We launched into a ridiculous argument about knowing and not knowing until I realized I was in no shape to navigate my way through a debate, either.

Our reactions were divergent, in a manner similar to what had happened after the miscarriage, only over a larger issue. The wedge was driven between us and would continue to push us further apart before we reconnected.

I'm not sure why I expected Dallas to understand how I felt when I didn't even understand. I hung up, still staring at the street, waiting for something to start making sense.

I couldn't find a single thought.

The sounds of the traffic began to fade.

I became fixated on a crack in the pavement without noticing any other sight or sound. Little did I realize, post-traumatic stress was settling in again and taking over.

I was numb.

I have no idea how long I stood there, staring at the ground, or how I managed to drive home.

A month later, I took Trent in for a day of examination by their psychologist, speech therapist and clinician. They tried to get him to respond to his name. He did not. They tried to get him to play pretend. He had no idea what it was. He didn't roll a ball back, nor point, nor push a toy car along the ground. He just picked up the car and handled it as if it were a block of wood.

The examiners asked questions, scribbled down notes, and then did more testing, poking and prodding of the test subject, my beautiful baby boy. It was such a bizarre feeling to have my son being treated like a science experiment. I knew it had to be done though, and I watched the inevitable taking shape.

Later we found out the official verdict: autism, severe in nearly every category.

A one-two punch.

The same week we learned about Trent's autism diagnosis, I received a call from a friend of mine from out of state. Michelle was concerned about a mutual friend of ours, Jody, who was going through a tough time. Michelle feared she might become suicidal. I decided to drive out and help in hopes that my concern for someone else might do both of us some good.

It wasn't the first time Jody had been suicidal. I met her in the early 90s when I volunteered to help Mormon women who were dealing with same-sex attraction. Jody was one of the first to call me. She and I kept in touch over the years while she returned to the LDS Church and then when she entered another lesbian relationship.

After spending years in that relationship, she decided she wanted to return to the Church again. She broke up with her girlfriend and moved out, and also went back to a professional therapist. Memories of severe sexual abuse she'd suffered as a child kept coming up. Tragically, the intensity of it all pushed her too far. She began to view suicide as a way to escape the memories.

I went out to help then, and stayed with Michelle. Jody's therapist had the two of us check her into a psychiatric ward at the hospital. The most unnerving part occurred with one of the staff counselors. He asked various questions while he obtained information, including Jody's religion and the fact that her most recent difficulty was leaving her girlfriend and lesbian relationships in general. As if on cue, he said, "Well, there's an obvious problem right there. Being a lesbian and being made to feel guilty by the Mormon Church."

To have someone make a supposed determination of the problem based on knowing two things and only speaking with someone for ten minutes is ridiculous, not to mention unprofessional. Feeling guilt for same-sex attractions while being Mormon is a common problem that does need to be addressed. However, many mental health professionals seem to assume that everyone in such a case should embrace a gay identity and leave the religion behind. They don't realize there are people who do better following a different path – one that is based on the teachings of The Church of Jesus Christ of Latter-day Saints. Or, based on other faiths or personal beliefs. One in which people choose not to act on their same-sex attractions, not to identify according to them, and seek to explore other possibilities.

Jody reported that the psychiatrist assigned to her made a similar diagnosis, in even less time.

It is certainly true that many people have been harmed because others have insisted they could change their sexual orientation if they just tried hard enough. Or, that they could be "cured" of their homosexuality.

On the other hand, I know plenty of people, including myself, who have been harmed by the tendency to insist that attraction for the same sex determines a person's identity and the only hope for true peace and fulfillment is to accept that gay identity and live life accordingly.

When I came back out to help Jody at Michelle's request, I realized she was suicidal again. I thought to take her to the same hospital. It was the only one she could go to because she didn't have insurance. But then she'd be with the same misguided staff.

As I tried to figure out what I should do, I sensed a voice saying, "If you leave her, she will die."

The only thing I could think of was to drive her out of state, to my house. So, we got in my car and headed south. While I was driving, Jody started looking for something sharp in the glove box that she could use to hurt herself. Then, she went to grab the wheel and almost drove us both off the road, at 75 miles per hour.

No one should be in a situation like that. If somebody is seriously suicidal, it can be a threat to everyone involved. 911 should be called immediately. However, I knew that calling 911 and having her go back to that same hospital and those same doctors would do her more harm than good. Plus, I could not ignore the message that kept repeating, "If you leave her, she will die."

As we approached Nevada, I realized there was no way I could take her to my house where she'd be with my family. That would put them in danger, too. So, I simply took one of the Vegas exits, filled the car up with gas, and headed west toward California. Even though it was the middle of the night, I couldn't think of anything else to do.

Jody finally calmed down and fell asleep as we crossed the Nevada/California border. I leaned my own seat back a bit as I drove and took a slow, deep, deliberate breath. I tried to let my guard down, but it wouldn't budge. I tried to force it down, telling myself Jody was asleep and neither one of our lives were currently being threatened.

It was no use. My sympathetic nervous system showed no sympathy at all. My guard remained on duty, undeterred, like the guards at Buckingham Palace. Post-traumatic stress had settled in and I was being hypervigilant.

I continued driving, with all systems maintaining full alert, whether I wanted them to or not. I kept heading west until we reached the Pacific Ocean. Then I pulled into a parking space at Newport Beach, parking on top of the sand that had drifted onto the road. It was 4:00 a.m.

I parked facing the ocean, then leaned my car seat all the way back and tried to fall asleep. I couldn't even calm down. My heart kept racing.

I soon gave up on sleep. I sat back up and took a look around. I saw a group of people walking out of a door under a hazy light obscured by the fog that had rolled in. They had a familiar party sway.

The scene evoked an unexpected response from me—a rush of gratitude. As crazy as my night had been, it seemed better than if I'd spent the night partying like those people. I said a short prayer to thank my Heavenly Father that I was clean and sober. That moment of gratitude was yet another tender mercy.

I got out of the car and stepped over to the beach. When I sat down, I instinctively started running my hands through the sand. I scooped up two handfuls and let the sand slowly sift through my fingers, falling as if it were in an hourglass. There was something soothing about it. Irresistibly so.

I sifted the sand again and again. The repetitive motion lulled me into a calm state, one that I desperately needed. My breathing slowed. The muscles in my arms and chest began to relax.

As I sifted more sand, my mind drifted further from the crisis I'd been in. It was such a reprieve from the constant hypervigilance I hadn't been able to shake. My response to the life-or-death situation combined with my son's autism diagnosis.

Next thing I knew, Jody woke up. Fortunately, she found the ocean to be a welcome sight and the sleep had done her some good. She said she wanted to go for a walk. So off she went across the beach, gradually disappearing into the fog. It was an eerie scene.

I started to panic when I thought that she might throw herself off the rocks and into the surf. Then I realized I just couldn't worry about her anymore. I became more concerned about the safety and sanity of the mother of my three children. That was as far as my concern could go by then.

Jody did return. I knew I was spent and decided to call in reinforcements. By the grace of God, Dana lived in California and also knew Jody. I called her and we went to Dana's place. I laid down for a nap while the two of them talked. I realized that I still wasn't going to fall asleep. It was my first hint as to how severely the trauma of Trent's diagnosis and Jody's suicidal spell were affecting my body and my mind. Never before in my life had I stayed awake for 30 hours straight and found it impossible to sleep. I was exhausted for sure, but not sleepy at all.

However, I wasn't aware of just how drastically it was starting to affect my whole life.

Puree.

The all-consuming hypervigilance would not ease up, even after Jody left. I was sleeping two or three hours every night. There was such a sense of foreboding. A feeling that some ominous something of unknown origin and unseen powers was lurking nearby, threatening to strike. Like I'd been watching a scary movie and just couldn't get to sleep. I started feeling a need to escape.

Logically, I knew there was no present danger. However,

the functioning of my conscious mind seemed to be severely impaired. I was stuck in a strange time warp where all threats—all trauma across my lifespan—were triggered and present in the moment. And the moment was stretching out for days, then weeks, then months.

PTSD is often misunderstood. People usually think of soldiers as the ones who suffer from post-traumatic stress because of war. Then the soldiers return home, only to find the events replayed in their minds. However, you don't have to be a soldier in order to experience PTSD. Any of life's traumas might set it in motion, and it can be tough to stop.

Fear is such a powerful emotion. It is difficult to express and escape from. The response to trauma that I'd learned best, the means of escape I'd used in the past, had been drugs and alcohol. I was surprised at the immediacy and intensity with which the desire to use struck again. I desperately wanted to self-medicate, even though it had been more than a decade since I'd used, and almost just as long since I'd struggled with the overwhelming desire to do so.

But when trauma struck again, so did the urge to drink and use drugs. It felt as though I'd never quit using. Twelve years of sobriety seemed to disappear into thin air.

That's when the Lord inspired me to call Diane, a woman from our ward who I didn't know very well. I immediately told Diane about what was going on, that I wanted to use, and that I needed help not to. Low and behold, Diane "just happened to be" a therapist. Again, someone was put into my life when I desperately needed help.

My lack of sleep combined with the adrenalin overdose put me in a state far beyond exhaustion. Added to that were the rigors of everyday life: caring for three children, being a loving partner in a marriage, and contributing substantially to the family income.

My mind and body became a living, breathing torture chamber.

The worst part, by far, was the fact that the anxiety and depression smothered my ability to feel the spirit. I'd taken great care over the years to find and regularly maintain a certain level of the spirit upon which I had come to depend. It was my daily bread and living water.

It felt like I was losing my faith as well as my mind. I was well aware of the fact that tragedy strikes everyone. No one is immune. But my recent trials and traumas seemed to have occurred precisely because I was being obedient. We'd had a third child because we knew it was God's will and part of the plan. I'd helped Jody because I knew that if I didn't, she would have died.

It had taken so much faith and work for me to become sober and reach the point where I was worthy to enter the temple. Then, to marry a man, and to have children – three of them.

I'd gone to great lengths to consider, then nurture, and finally embrace all of it. I'd put in my time. I'd done it all in faith. I'd submitted to God's will. I'd taken advantage of the Atonement of Jesus Christ in miraculous ways.

So, how could all of this really be God's will? My beautiful baby boy being tortured. Helping a suicidal friend who should have been able to receive proper care in a hospital. Having my hard-earned years of sobriety threatened.

Not only did it seem unfair, which I had come to expect,

it also seemed to be a gross miscalculation on God's part. He promised He wouldn't give us more than we could bear. But this was definitely more than I could bear.

God had made a mistake. And if He was supposed to be perfect and all knowing, how could he have made such an obvious error in judgment?

He had grossly overestimated my capacity. Because, try as I might, I could not pull myself together. I discovered that it's impossible to pull yourself up by your bootstraps when you can't even *find* your bootstraps.

The combined traumas, the lack of sleep, the relentless desire to escape using drugs or alcohol, my smothered faith. Everything together sent me into a tailspin. A downward spiral that gained more and more momentum until everything seemed to get stuck on puree.

The Great Divide.

Our marriage was affected by everything that was going on, too. Dallas had an entirely different response to Trent's autism. He accepted it as part of God's plan–difficult, to be sure, but part of a greater plan. He was also certain Trent would be fine.

I couldn't understand how Dallas could be so calm when tragedy had struck our family. How could he feel so certain Trent would be fine when he was severely autistic? Didn't he care about our son?

Dallas couldn't understand why I was so distraught. As I began to crumble under the weight of it all, he thought I was just making it all about me. He wondered how I could be so certain Trent was in so much trouble. Didn't I care enough about our son and our two daughters to pull myself out of my anxiety and pain?

After nine years of marriage, we had come to our first major divide. From opposite ends of the precipice, we couldn't see or understand each other's side.

While we struggled, Dallas was asked to teach a couple of Institute classes. I asked him not to. I wanted him home in case I was having a hard time and needed help with the kids.

Dallas felt it was important for him to teach Institute, to put the Lord first.

I insisted that putting his family first was part of putting the Lord first.

Dallas thought I was being selfish and that I was making Trent's problem all about me.

I was shocked that he could be so oblivious, or perhaps even uncaring, with regard to the pain I was in.

As we continued to argue, I collapsed in tears, begging Dallas not to teach. I desperately cried out that I needed help, as I was writhing in pain, curled up on the floor in the fetal position.

I was beside myself, finding it impossible to believe what was happening. Here was this man, my husband, to whom I had been sealed in the temple, the only man I ever trusted enough and loved enough to marry, and he was tromping on my heart in heavy boots while seeming not to care. So much for removing his shoes while walking on sacred ground.

How could I be married to a man I couldn't trust? That thought triggered something else traumatic—my distrust of men stemming from the sexual abuse. I could not be in the same house with a man I didn't trust. That didn't come as a thought; rather, as a deep-rooted feeling. I felt I needed to protect myself. I didn't think I was safe. I had to get away.

I went into the bedroom to grab a pair of pajamas, a toothbrush and clothes. I had no idea where I was going and it didn't matter. It was leaving that was so important, not arriving. I wanted to escape, to find safety somewhere, away from this man who couldn't be trusted.

I'm certain the Lord stepped in and inspired Dallas to come in and apologize. I apologized, too, but something had been disturbed deep within me that I knew I'd need to remedy at some point. There was far too much to deal with for me to choose any one thing.

I was back in the frozen trauma place, except now it had become a deep freeze.

Gratefully, Dallas was inspired to call his father to find out what he thought about his teaching Institute versus staying home in case I needed help. His father recommended putting the family first. Dallas followed his counsel. Bless his dad, and bless Dallas for listening to him.

The lone coyote howl.

When parents are deeply affected by something, it tends to spread throughout the family. Autism is one of those diagnoses that affects the whole family. Dallas, Trent and I weren't the only ones struggling. All of our children showed signs of struggle.

Marie felt the loss, to be sure. She was born with the mothering instinct times ten (go figure) and had grown so attached to Trent. As she commented later, looking back: "It was like I lost a little brother. I had this happy, smiling baby brother and the next thing I knew, he was crying all the time and biting and kicking me. I thought 'Where did my sweet little baby brother go?'"

She also lost the close relationship with her mother. I felt the need to spend a lot of time alone as I tried to cope. Or, I'd spend time working.

Ann started suffering a heightened sense of the middle child syndrome. Up until that point, Dallas and I had been pretty good at spreading our love and attention wide to include all three kids fairly equally. Now, I had very little left to give anyone.

I used what energy and focus I did have to try and find ways to treat Trent's autism. He was diagnosed a few years before autism hit the media and rates like 1 in 150, then 1 in 100 were being reported.

Trent continued to become more distant and more frustrated. I hated being unable to help. With most kids, not counting Marie, it's somewhat predictable. They either need to be changed or fed or held. But Trent would scream and cry and I couldn't find a way to console him, no matter what I did. He didn't want to be held, which was especially difficult. I was willing to bounce him all day like we did Marie, if only it would help. But he wouldn't tolerate it.

He'd cry, then I'd cry. His distress became mine.

His budding vocabulary had stopped growing and then withered on the vine. His animal sounds died off, one by one. First the duck, then the pig, the sheep, the cow, and even the fish (puckered lips opening and closing).

The coyote managed to hang on the longest. A lone call in a vast wasteland of forgotten syllables.

Faced with the threat of losing all communication, I held onto his coyote call for dear life. I'd ask him again and again, just to feel reassured by a response. Any response.

"What does the coyote say?"

"Ahh-oooooo."

All other requests fell on deaf ears, or silent lips, or misfiring brain, or whatever else had stricken our baby boy.

Eventually, the last audible connection between mother and son, a faint "ah-oooo," faded into the sunset.

To this day, I can still hear the haunting echo of his final coyote call.

Along with sounds went communication of any kind: looking up when we called his name, direct eye contact, reaching up to be held. He also began spinning around in circles even more, acting as if he were in his own world, rotating around his axis, in his own universe.

One day I couldn't get his attention at all, no matter what I did. I'd poured him a bowl of cereal. He just stared off into space. Usually he'd eat food when it was placed in front of him. I knew he was hungry, but he wouldn't even look at the cereal. Or at me.

"Trent look, it's Kix. Remember, you love Kix!"

Nothing.

My heart raced and pulse quickened as I began to panic. I scooped up a spoonful of cereal and held it right in front of his face.

"Trent!"

Nothing.

I put the spoon up to my own mouth and pretended to eat. "Mmm, yumm. I love Kix. Don't you want some?"

Still nothing.

Then I started making sounds and motions like the spoon was the Jetson's spaceship getting louder with each approach toward his mouth, then quieter as it circled round. That used to make him laugh – really hard – with this adorable belly laugh of his. That had disappeared along with the duck and the pig. I panicked even more when I realized just how long it had been since I'd heard Trent laugh.

I ducked behind the cereal box and started playing what turned out to be peek-a-boo solitaire.

"Peek-a-boo."

No response.

I stuck my head around the other side of the box.

"Peek-a-boo."

No response again.

I ducked beneath the counter and popped back up.

"Peek-a-boo."

No response the third time, so I screamed, "PEEK-A-BOO." Apparently, I would have even settled for a startle response. That's how desperate I was to get some sort of reaction from my son.

Nothing.

Trent looked around, but not at me.

With the intensity and determination of a platoon leader, I got right in front of his face. "Trent! Trent! Look, at me. It's your mother! It's me!"

My voice cracked and softened as I lost my platoon leader composure. "I'm your mom. Remember me?"

I realized I was staring at a face I didn't recognize, either. The familiar sparkle in Trent's eyes was gone.

Then a thought was detonated: What if I can't ever reach my son again?

His brilliant little spirit had disappeared into the shell of his body. I tried to reach in and pull him out, to save him, but I was helpless to help. The intensity of desperation and despair was shocking.

Sounds turned distant. My legs began to gel. I grabbed the kitchen counter for support as numbness set in.

Then I was pulled back into action when I realized I still had a child in danger.

Nothing affects a mother like a threat to her child. My sympathetic nervous system sprung into action, pouring adrenalin into my bloodstream by the bucketfuls. Time slowed to a near halt as my mind sifted through a lifetime of experiences to find the best response, the best way to help my child in this apparent emergency situation.

I'm sure that a beyond-conscious spiritual intuition aroused itself, too, linking generations of mothers past to help generations of mothers here and those yet to come.

Then I thought to take Trent to his dad to see if he'd respond to him. I grabbed him from his highchair and ran out to the car, clutching him to my chest with his head held tightly against my shoulder. I flung open the car door, put him in back and strapped him into his car seat. Then I rushed over to where my husband was working. I'm not sure exactly why I thought it was such an emergency. We had been gradually approaching this place of horror.

Dallas was standing out front when we arrived. I jumped out of the car while pushing out words as fast as I could. "Dallas, I can't get Trent's attention, at all! I've tried everything! He won't even look at me. See if he'll look at you! Please, see if he'll look at you!"

Dallas got in the car and tried as earnestly as I did.

He was equally unsuccessful.

"It's like we aren't even here! It's like he isn't even here! He's gone!"

My face formed strange contortions as I hung on the verge of tears, not purposefully holding back but unable to move beyond the brink because I was so numb. Without uttering another word, I got back into the car.

I drove around town with the empty shell of my boy strapped into the car seat in back. It was like my son had molted and his spirit had taken off, leaving nothing but an exoskeleton in size 2T jeans, a brown polo shirt, and a pair of blue sneakers.

I'd read plenty about regressive autism. However, there are no words on earth or in heaven that can prepare a parent for the harsh surreality of it all. It's one thing to read about autism. It's quite another to stand by and watch, helplessly, as it turns your bright, bubbly little boy into something entirely foreign.

I've heard of mothers who accidentally leave their child strapped in the car seat, with dire consequences. Trent was the one who seemed to have left his own small body in the car seat. The consequences seemed almost as tragic.

Shots in the dark.

Having survived the torment of homosexual attractions and desires to abuse drugs and alcohol that were pitted against an undeniable testimony, I'd assumed I had endured the worst suffering of my life. What I hadn't counted on was the depth and breadth of the suffering a mother endures when disaster strikes one of her children. Especially when she feels helpless to help.

"Take me! Mess me up if you must! But please, not one of my children!"

Something had to be done for Trent, right away. But what? We had tried the infamous gluten-free casein-free (GFCF) diet, known to help a few kids with autism. Unfortunately, Trent wasn't one of them.

The only thing the GFCF diet did was make life more difficult for our family. You don't realize how many foods have gluten, or casein, or both, until you start checking. Not only is gluten found in wheat, it's in fully bleached, fully processed, unrecognizable derivatives of wheat. Cheetos, Doritos, even French fries, for heaven's sake. Not to mention other grains like rye, barley, and oats.

We had to eliminate cereals, pasta, pizza, cake, cookies, bread, bagels, and hamburger buns. Even unlikely foods like various candy, soup, and soy sauce. And those are just the gluten-free foods. Add casein-free and you've got to get rid of cow's milk plus other dairy favorites like cheese, yogurt and ice cream.

It's ironic. Parents who are exhausted and overwhelmed by an autism diagnosis end up hunting for suspect proteins in every food their kids might possibly eat. To complicate matters, kids on the autism spectrum are notoriously picky eaters. Even when you let them choose from any and all foods known to humankind.

We kept up the diet for as long as we could. After eating

bread made of gravel, or something that tasted like it, and omitting nearly every food our family was used to eating, we finally concluded that the GFCF diet was ineffective for Trent and miserable for the rest of us.

The huge drawback to stopping the diet, however, was that again we had to stand by and watch, helplessly, not doing anything as Trent disappeared from our family.

One evening, I attended a group meeting for parents with children on the autism spectrum, hoping I might find some ideas about how to help. A doctor who specialized in kids with autism spoke, discussing Applied Behavior Analysis (ABA) programs and talking about some of the difficulties with extreme autism cases. After his lecture, he invited the audience to ask questions. Ask they did.

One woman had a girl with autism who would make herself vomit when she wanted attention. Another parent's child wore a protective helmet at all times because he constantly beat his head against the wall. Another child had to wear diapers still, at age 12, and after he defecated he'd wipe the feces all over the walls. One mother reported watching helplessly as her son paced and walked in circles all day long, pitching a fit every once in a while, with absolutely no acknowledgment of anyone around him. He was 15 years old.

As parents continued to comment, I slumped down in my chair like I was made of soft wax. Trent's future, our entire family's future, looked terribly bleak as seen through the eyes of these tortured parents.

Unfortunately, the meeting added to my hopelessness and despair. Dallas was troubled by it. I was devastated by it.

The next few days I prayed for help but the depression

and darkness were so severe, I couldn't feel the light of the Spirit at all. I struggled just to get from the bed to the floor to begin the day.

So many years had passed since I'd faced persistent depression and anxiety. This time, though, I was living the gospel standards and remaining worthy of a temple recommend. It took every ounce of strength to do so. To remain sober through it all. I never thought I'd have to go back to those temptations if I remained obedient long enough. According to my timetable, I'd put plenty of time in.

I relearned a lesson I'd apparently forgotten. The Lord does not use the same timetable as we do. In fact, I suspect He has no timetable at all. It's just a human device of measurement, and a terribly inaccurate one at that.

I also learned, in painfully new ways, that obedience does not always equal peace and happiness. And it doesn't always mean that old temptations won't rear their ugly heads again.

On the wings of angels.

Another of the Lord's tender mercies took place that Halloween. And oh, how I was in need of a tender mercy.

Our neighborhood was having a Halloween picnic at the park before trick or treating. I'd gotten a little bee costume for Trent. When I started to put it on him, he fussed. Dressing him in regular clothes was a chore. Putting on the bee suit was next to impossible.

Dallas walked by as Trent was crying and asked, "Why are you putting a costume on him? He doesn't want one."

"Let me just see if he'll wear it." I knew Dallas was probably right, but I couldn't squelch my desire to have

Trent seem like all the other kids – even if I had to dress him up like a bee to do it.

"I don't want him to be the only kid on Halloween that doesn't have a costume. Can't he be like all the other kids for just one night?"

Dallas walked off, shaking his head in disapproval. Tears ran down my face as I finished turning Trent into a bee. He calmed down once I got the costume on him, even letting me put the headband with antennae on his head. Finally, he was ready to go to the Halloween party incognito as a typical kid.

He started flicking the wings on his back. Maybe he liked them. It was impossible to tell. I knew he didn't hate them, though. He would have been screaming bloody murder if he hated them.

We all headed up the street: our little bee, the gypsy whose wild hair kept getting stuck in her huge dangling earrings, and our Elizabethan bride, with her perfect posture, in a billowy dress that puffed up and out as she floated over the asphalt (luckily she didn't get her posture from me).

At the park, we had hot dogs and homemade root beer. Afterward, most of the adults sat around talking while the kids played on the playground. Dallas took Trent over to the swing set.

Swinging was one of the few things Trent seemed to like. It was probably the repetitive motion, the lulling back and forth. There was another father and son pair using the swing next to them. The boy was dressed up as an M&M. Apparently, big round M&M's don't swing too well because they were having quite a time of it. Our little bee fit just fine into the swing, after Dallas managed to untangle his wing from the chain.

As the swing began its back and forth motion, higher and higher, Trent got this big smile on his face. It had been a long time since I'd seen any facial expression from him, much less a smile. The M&M swinging next to him did not look nearly so content. Other kids in costumes were playing nearby, running around yelling and laughing.

Somehow, for that slice of time, Trent really did seem like all the other kids. I never thought I'd be so excited to have my child seem so average.

Then I noticed that every time Trent swung back and started to swing forward again, his little wings would catch some air and spread out wide. It looked as though he were flying. And instead of a bee, he looked like an angel descending from heaven, with a radiant smile on his face.

A sense of peace descended upon me with the kind of power only the divine can bear sway. As my littlest angel flew through the air, smiling as wide as the universe, I received a powerful witness that Trent would not always be trapped in that mortal mind and body hindered by autism. There would come a day, in this life or the next, when he would soar like an angel.

Later that evening, Dallas took Trent trick or treating to a couple of houses while I took the girls to every door in the neighborhood, and the next neighborhood over. When we came home loaded with overstuffed trick or treat bags, we found Dallas and Trent fast asleep on the couch, clothes, bee costume and all.

One of Trent's little wings was tucked between them and one antenna stuck straight up. Dallas' arm was tenderly wrapped around him, with his left hand resting on Trent's chest, just above his heart.

As I approached, the light from the floor lamp reflected off of Dallas' wedding band. The same ring I'd placed on his fourth finger. The one with the legendary venus amoris, the vein of love, that no doubt ran directly from Trent's heart to Dallas' heart to mine. And then to heaven.

I thought of my favorite scripture at the end of that day. A day I'd need to call to heart many times in the future.

"How excellent is thy lovingkindness, O God! therefore the children of men put their trust under the shadow of thy wings."[6]

EPILOGUE

In October of 2011, a producer from LDS Public Affairs contacted me and asked if I'd be willing to be filmed for a website that the Church was putting together. They wanted to help increase understanding about same-sex attraction. After some hesitation, I called the producer back and agreed to be filmed. The website was released in December of 2012. Three days later, the Deseret News ran an article about me as a participant on the website.

The article read:

For Laurie Campbell, it is time to come forward.

"I've never really wanted to be this visible," she said during a recent telephone interview. "I have children. I have a life. I have a few of my family members and friends who still don't know much about my history. I don't know how they'll respond now."

Still, she knew she needed to come forward and participate in the new website, mormonsandgays.org, launched Thursday by The Church of Jesus Christ of Latter-day Saints. You'll see her in several of the website's video sequences, sharing her thoughts and feelings along with other church leaders and members, urging compassion, acceptance, love, and empathy between

Latter-day Saints and those who experience same-sex attraction.

With all her heart, she believes God requires this of her.

"It's time," she says quietly. "My husband and I thought and prayed about this a lot when the church approached me a year ago to be interviewed for the website. We feel it's time for me to come forward and be more vocal."

So here she is, coming forward as a happily married 52-year-old mother of three who, 30 years ago, was living her life as a lesbian.

"We knew this was going to be a church website, so we figured our family and friends would see it," she said Friday. "The thing is, I hadn't told my kids about my past yet, and we just moved into a new ward. And I'm thinking, 'yeah, we're going to be telling everybody to come look at this website where I talk about the sins I committed.'"

The filming process was sensitively handled, she felt, and talking to her children about it was a sweet experience.

"After talking to my oldest daughter, I asked her if she was going to be embarrassed by having me on a church website talking about my experiences with same-gender attraction, and she said, 'I'm not embarrassed. I'm proud of you for doing it,'" Campbell said. "My youngest daughter was like, 'Oh sure, no problem.'

It was no big deal to her."

Campbell has told her story before, in a book published by Deseret Book in 1994 called "Born That Way?" She has spoken about her experiences at several annual conferences of Evergreen International, an independent organization that focuses on same-sex attraction from within the perspective of the doctrines, teachings and policies of The Church of Jesus Christ of Latter-day Saints. She also has a blog with North Star, a website for Latter-day Saints dealing with issues surrounding homosexual attraction.

But for the most part she has remained behind the scenes, often using her pen name, Erin Eldridge.

Now she is coming forward using her own name and being shown on camera in the new website, with hopes that the story of her journey will give hope to others who find themselves feeling trapped between their sexual orientation and their LDS beliefs.

"I'm not trying to win an argument here, or to change anyone's mind who has found happiness and peace with their sexual orientation, whatever it may be," she said. "I'm reaching out to those who are not happy with their orientation, who don't want to be gay, and who want to free themselves from overwhelming desires that create conflict."

To them, she says, her message is simple: "There is hope."

And the best way for her to deliver that message, she

believes, is through telling her own story, using her own name.

"I don't want Latter-day Saints with same-sex attraction to feel ashamed to tell other church members about what they're dealing with or have dealt with," she said. "It is so important to open up to others, to feel supported, loved and accepted. I'm hoping that by appearing on the website and talking about my experiences openly it will help others do so in more private settings."

And because of the message of the site, she hopes others can speak about their feelings to family members, church leaders and friends in an environment of increased love, understanding and support . . .

"We need to be empathetic, especially with young people, and try to understand what they're going through. Everyone's journey is different," she continued. "I'm trying to help those who are attracted to the same sex, who choose not to self-identify as gay, and want to work toward marriage as best they can. They feel it is important to hope for a future family, where they can be married as husband and wife, serving as father and mother in the home. And if not in this life, certainly in the eternities."

Campbell acknowledges that not every Mormon who experiences same-sex attraction feels that way. But many do.

"The message they get from the world is that the only option you have is to accept these feelings, that to do otherwise is to deny who you are," she said. "There is no room in that mindset to consider other possibilities. You're just supposed to accept it . . .

"I don't identify as gay or ex-gay, heterosexual or bisexual. I identify as a daughter of God," Campbell said. "Some people don't realize that we choose our identity. It isn't heaped upon us, uncontrollably. I'm not sure you can completely change your orientation. But what I am sure of, because I have experienced it and know others who have, is that it's possible to change from a person who is only attracted to the same gender to a person who, at some point in their lives, is able to fall in love with someone of the opposite gender," she continued. "And you can be happy and at peace in your marriage, with your children and with your faith."

"I'm not saying things will turn out this way for everyone," Campbell says. "And when it comes right down to it, that's not even the most important thing. Elder (Neal A.) Maxwell said that the Lord wants us to sacrifice our will to his. He wants us to turn our hearts and lives over to him and say, 'Do with me what you will.'

"For those with same-sex attraction, that means telling the Lord, 'If I am never to get married in this life, I'm willing to remain single. And if I am to be married, I trust you will help me be attracted to someone I can marry.' That's what happened for me."

"There's nothing homophobic or hateful about wanting to change," Campbell said. "Just as we need to reach out with sincere Christ-like love and respect to those who are gay, we also need to reach out to those who don't want to be gay and offer love, encouragement and support."

And hope. Lots of hope.[1]

Marvel not that all mankind must be born again.

I have been a proponent of the mighty change for more than 20 years. That's because the gospel of Jesus Christ of Latter-day Saints not only encourages a mighty change – a spiritual rebirth – it is a commandment. The scriptures reiterate the importance of faith, repentance, baptism by water when the natural self is buried, and then the baptism of fire and the Holy Ghost when we're purified and become spiritually reborn. This is also referred to as becoming born of God, becoming children of Christ, sanctification, becoming converted, and being quickened in the inner man.

"Marvel not that all mankind ... must be born again; yea, born of God, changed from their carnal and fallen state, to a state of righteousness, being redeemed of God, becoming his sons and daughters; and thus they become new creatures."[2]

Modern day prophets and apostles have joined in the clarion call for spiritual rebirth. During the past ten years at General Conference, they have underscored its importance more frequently than ever before.

Elder David R. Bednar states, "We are instructed to 'come unto Christ, and be perfected in him, and deny [ourselves] of all ungodliness', to become 'new creature[s]' in

Christ, to put off 'the natural man', and to experience 'a mighty change in us, or in our hearts, that we have no more disposition to do evil, but to do good continually'. Please note that the conversion described in these verses is mighty, not minor – a spiritual rebirth and fundamental change of what we feel and desire, what we think and do, and what we are. Indeed, the essence of the gospel of Jesus Christ entails a fundamental and permanent change in our very nature ... As we choose to follow the Master, we choose to be changed – to be spiritually reborn."[3]

Whatever our weaknesses and sins, the process of the mighty change is the same. Christ promises to help turn our weaknesses into strengths if we will deny ourselves of all ungodliness.[4] As we do all we can, unrighteous desires of the natural self are changed through the transformative, healing power of Jesus Christ.

King Benjamin tells his massive congregation of active Church members that "the natural man is an enemy to God ... and will be, forever and ever, unless he yields to the enticings of the Holy Spirit, and putteth off the natural man."[5] They believe his words and declare: "the Spirit of the Lord Omnipotent has wrought a mighty change in us, or in our hearts, that we have no more disposition to do evil, but to do good continually."[6]

The pull of the carnal, natural self with its sinful desires creates dissonance between the body and spirit. In search of immediate relief from our dis-ease, we become tempted to "self-medicate" in whatever ways the natural self desires:

pornography, drugs, lustful thoughts, inappropriate relationships, gambling, and so on. The adversary offers a wide variety of counterfeits from which to choose.

With enough repetition, fostering sinful desires and committing sinful acts can become bad habits, pernicious addictions, and even a false sense of identity. We may then conclude that our sinful desires are so much a part of us, so heavily entrenched despite fervent efforts to overcome, that there is no hope for change.

But that is Satan's lie. He seeks to have us and hold us captive by convincing us that our sinful desires are somehow permanent. His counterfeits often *feel* spiritually correct because spiritual needs are being met: a desire for love, a sense of belonging, relief from depression or pain, or an escape from the stress of everyday life or traumatic events.

Just because the needs are righteous, that doesn't mean they are being met in righteous ways.

To prove ourselves worthy, we must be willing to endure the depression, anxiety, and other uncomfortable feelings that contribute to our dependencies. Over time, such desires and cravings will dissipate. However, they can also reappear in varying waves of intensity, causing us to think we haven't changed at all. Instead of giving up or giving in, it's important to press forward in faith—even if we lapse or relapse.

The Lord's way, the straight and narrow, requires faithful obedience while holding fast to the word of God. We are to be "patient in afflictions"[7] and remain willing "to submit to all things which the Lord seeth fit to inflict" upon us.[8]

It is neither fast nor easy. And, from the limited, myopic vision of our natural eyes, we may see it as unnecessary, or too difficult, or even impossible.

From a gospel perspective, "The Lord's way is not hard. Life is hard, not the gospel. 'There is an opposition in all things,' everywhere, for everyone. Life is hard for all of us, but life is also simple. We have only two choices. We can either follow the Lord and be endowed with His power and have peace, light, strength, knowledge, confidence, love, and joy, or we can go some other way, any other way, whatever other way, and go it alone – without His support, without His power, without guidance, in darkness, turmoil, doubt, grief, and despair. And I ask, which way is easier?"[9]

We need to starve the natural self to death. The resulting hunger pangs can be difficult to endure, especially when immediate satisfaction is close at hand. Growing accustomed to nourishment the Lord's way takes time. Eventually, it provides a depth and breadth of gratification that causes those who become filled with the Holy Spirit to wonder how Satan's counterfeits ever seemed so real.

The counterfeits may work for a time, but certainly not forever. For those who seek satisfaction outside the Lord's boundaries, "it shall be unto them, even as unto a hungry man which dreameth, and behold he eateth but he awaketh and his soul is empty; or like unto a thirsty man which dreameth, and behold he drinketh but he awaketh and behold he is faint, and his soul hath appetite."[10]

The Lord provides that which satisfies. "There is only

one way to happiness and fulfilment. He is the Way. Every other way, any other way, whatever other way, is *madness*. He offers a well of living water. Either we drink and never thirst more, or we don't and foolishly remain thirsty still. He is the Bread of Life. Either we eat and hunger no more, or we don't and foolishly remain weak and hungry still."[11]

Christ has traveled the path before us. He is the Way. He has already been where we are. He went forth "suffering pains and afflictions and temptations of every kind…that he may know according to the flesh how to succor his people according to their infirmities."[12] He stands ready to comfort and heal us as we go through our personal Gethsemanes.

Change is most effective when we turn to Christ and change at a spiritual level. If it takes place at a temporal level only, we may stop the behavior for a time, but our desires don't usually change much. Then we're constantly battling urges and cravings in an effort to avoid the resultant behavior, which often causes us to give in.

By redirecting our lives spiritually and experiencing change at the deepest level, the temporal will follow – " First spiritual, secondly temporal." [13]

I emphasize the spiritual aspect of change because that is the most critical and enduring. For "no temporal commandment gave I unto him, for my commandments are spiritual; they are not natural nor temporal, neither carnal nor sensual."[14]

We must begin by following the Savior and the Holy Spirit. Elder Jeffrey R. Holland spoke to "those who endure conflicts fought in the lonely foxholes of the heart, those trying to hold back floodwaters of despair that sometimes wash over us like a tsunami of the soul . . ."

"Are you battling a demon of addiction–tobacco or drugs or gambling, or the pernicious contemporary plague of pornography? . . . Are you confused with gender identity or searching for self-esteem? . . . Whatever other steps you may need to take to resolve these concerns, come first to the gospel of Jesus Christ. Trust in Heaven's promises. In that regard Alma's testimony is my testimony: 'I do know,' he says, 'that whosoever shall put their trust in God shall be supported in their trials, and their troubles, and their afflictions.'"[15]

If there have been past failures, then growth and change may seem impossible. However, with help from God, "all things are possible."[16] Elder Lawrence E. Corbridge testifies that, "while the Lord's invitation to follow Him is the highest of all, it is also achievable by everyone, not because we are able, but because He is, and because He can make us able too. "[17]

It is the transforming power of the Atonement of Jesus It is the transforming power of the Atonement of Jesus Christ that will enable us to put off the natural man and feel "the enticings of the Holy Spirit"[18] rather than being enticed by sin. Entice means to tempt or lure. Imagine feeling tempted to follow the Spirit and finding it difficult to resist. Our minds would become filled with spiritual thoughts and enticing images of doing good. We would look for moments when we could sneak away to perform secret acts of kindness.

Obedience would require less effort because that would be what we truly desire. And that is so much easier than constantly trying not to think about doing something bad.

The mighty change of heart enables us to become "of one heart and of one soul"[19] with Jesus Christ, Heavenly Father, and the other Saints who have been born again. This is especially important for those of us who would like to be a part of the gathering of Zion – the New Jerusalem – in these, the latter days.

The city of Enoch, which was taken up to heaven, was called Zion because the people "were of one heart and one mind, and dwelt in righteousness."[20]

During Joseph Smith's time, the Saints did try to establish Zion in Missouri, but failed to uphold its high standards. The Lord explains why they fell short: "they have not learned to be obedient to the things which I required at their hands" and they "are not united according to the union required by the law of the celestial kingdom."[21]

He discusses it further: "there were jarrings, and contentions, and envyings, and strifes, and lustful and covetous desires among them; therefore by these things they polluted their inheritances."[22]

Elder D. Todd Christofferson admonishes us: "Remember, 'the Lord called his people Zion, because they were of one heart and one mind, and dwelt in righteousness . . . It will be necessary to become unified in one heart and one mind; to become, individually and collectively, a holy people . . ."

"We cannot wait until Zion comes for these things to

happen – Zion will come only as they happen."

So, "let us seek to build up Zion through unity, godliness, and charity, preparing for that great day when Zion, the New Jerusalem, will arise."[23]

It is not the physical gathering; rather, it is the spiritual gathering of Zion in these latter days with which we should concern ourselves. Church membership and rote obedience alone will not suffice. Our hearts must literally be in it, without reservation. We are to convert, turning away from our old ways and toward Zion, unflinchingly, without looking back upon our past sins longingly. Lot's wife made that mistake, with catastrophic results.

In order to be of one heart, we need to love one another, including our family, friends, and enemies. Including those who experience serious transgressions, addictions, and homosexual attractions as well as those who are critical or judgmental of such people.

With outstretched arms.

Looking back over my life, it is evident that my faith-turned-to-knowledge and my relationship with the Savior gained incalculable strength when I sacrificed lesbian relationships and addictions. Sacrifices like that can yield great results. I never would have made it through everything else in my life without the blessings brought forth from those sacrifices. Namely, a mighty change of heart.

I cannot calculate all that I have learned and all that I am because of the law of sacrifice and the principle of spiritual rebirth. I consider the life I live now to be well worth it. I also feel that I have so much precisely because of what I've given up and endured along the way.

Many outside of the LDS Church, and even some within our ranks, have been critical of Church leaders for expecting those people with homosexual attractions to become "something they are not."

We are not asked to become something we're not; rather, to become something we truly are—Latter-day Saints so faithful that we are willing to sacrifice all that is required to undergo a mighty change and follow the gospel plan. This holds true for any life or sin the natural man desires.

To those who criticize Church leaders, I would object similarly to one of the men who survived the pioneer trek with the Willie and Martin Handcart Company.

Some were criticizing Church leadership for sending the company out so late in the season. The man stood up in the middle of Sunday School class and defended the Church. He spoke of how the Lord was with them on their journey and summed everything up with, "The price we paid to become acquainted with God was a privilege to pay."[24]

I can relate to his story. I recall many times when I was so weak and weary from working hard to be obedient, or to try and be obedient, that I felt I could not take another step. I looked ahead, to the end of a day and thought, "I think I can make it through today, but then I simply must give up. I cannot carry this load any longer." Then, when I reached the end of that day, I was somehow carried through to the next day. And the next. And the next. And as I look back, I know angels were there helping me.

The price I have paid to become acquainted with God has been a privilege to pay. The journey has been difficult, but not impossible.

There is always hope, even if it takes a while to find it.

In the October 2006 General Conference, Elder Holland said: "To all of you who think you are lost or without hope, or who think you have done too much that was too wrong for too long, to every one of you who worry that you are stranded somewhere on the wintry plains of life and have wrecked your handcart in the process, this conference calls out Jehovah's unrelenting refrain, '[My] hand is stretched out still.' 'I shall lengthen out mine arm unto them,' He said, '[and even if they] deny me; nevertheless, I will be merciful unto them . . . if they will repent and come unto me; for mine arm is lengthened out all the day long, saith the Lord God of Hosts.' His mercy endureth forever, and His hand is stretched out still. His is the pure love of Christ, the charity that never faileth, that compassion which endures even when all other strength disappears."[25]

For those who are still wandering out there on the frozen plains, remember that there is hope. For those of us who are currently living more comfortable lives, Christ asks us to go out and help those in need.

There are people looking for support and acceptance from somewhere other than the places they are trying to leave behind. We are to welcome them and not alienate them. They need a sense of belonging and we, as Christ's disciples, can surely provide it. We should reserve judgment and suspend foregone conclusions. The Lord is in charge, and we are his servants.

As Elder Holland states in that same conference address, "It may not be blizzards and frozen-earth burials that we face this conference, but the needy are still out there–the poor and the weary, the discouraged and downhearted, those '[falling] away into [the] forbidden paths' we mentioned earlier, and multitudes who are 'kept from the truth because they know not where to find it.' They are all out there with feeble knees, hands that hang down, and bad weather setting in. They can be rescued only by those who have more and know more and can help more. And don't worry about asking, 'Where are they?' They are everywhere, on our right hand and on our left, in our neighborhoods and in the workplace, in every community and county and nation of this world."[26]

Those who struggle with any trial need our attention, our compassion, and our outstretched arms–no matter how difficult the trial is to comprehend, and even if we don't agree with a person's life choices. I do not know of anyone who has returned to the fold because their family or friends rejected them. The opposite is true, most especially with the youth. Rejection often contributes to depression, low self-esteem, homelessness, and even suicide.

I would not be where I am today were it not for the support of my family, friends, and Church leaders. I struggled with serious transgression, but I was not beyond the reach of the Lord. Nobody is. There is hope for everyone, no matter how lost we think they are, or they think they are.

This is God's work, after all, and He is a God of miracles. My life is a witness of that.

NOTES

Introduction

1. Mosiah 3:19.
2. David A. Bednar, CES Devotional delivered at the University of Texas at Arlington, March 3, 2013.
3. "Repentance," LDS Bible Dictionary, 760.
4. Mosiah 3:19.
5. "Repentance," LDS Bible Dictionary, 760.
6. Helaman 15:7.
7. Alma 22:15–16, 18.
8. David A. Bednar, "Clean Hands and a Pure Heart," *Ensign*, November 2007, 82.
9. 1 Corinthians 2:14.
10. 2 Corinthians 5:17.
11. Acts 21:13.
12. Bruce R. McConkie, Address delivered at the University of Utah, Salt Lake City, January 10, 1982.
13. David A. Bednar, "The Atonement and the Journey of Mortality," *Ensign*, April 2012, 44.
14. Ezra T. Benson, "Born of God," *Ensign*, November 1985, 6.
15. David A. Bednar, "We Believe in Being Chaste," *Ensign*, April 2013, 42.

Mighty Change I

1. Ephesians 6: 12.
2. "O My Father," *Hymns of The Church of Jesus Christ of Latter-day Saints* [Salt Lake City: The Church of Jesus Christ of Latter-day Saints, 1985], 292.
3. D&C 46: 13.
4. 3 Nephi 9: 20.
5. "When He Comes Again," *Children's Songbook of The Church of Jesus Christ of Latter-day Saints* [Salt Lake City: The Church of Jesus Christ of Latter-day Saints, 2002], 82.
6. Isaiah 40: 12.
7. Hebrews 11: 1.
8. Spencer W. Kimball, *Hidden Wedges* [Salt Lake City: Deseret Book Co., 1974], 1.
9. *Ibid.,* 2–3.
10. Wray Herbert, "Embattled Childhood: The Real Trauma in PTSD," *Scientific American Mind,* November/December 2012, 74-75.
11. Elder Neal A. Maxwell, *We Will Prove Them Herewith* [Salt Lake City: Deseret Book Co., 1982], 24.
12. Daniel Farson, *Sacred Monsters* [London: Bloomsbury Publishing, 1990].
13. D&C 121: 45
14. "We Thank Thee, O God, For a Prophet" *Hymns of The Church of Jesus Christ of Latter-day Saints* [Salt Lake City: The Church of Jesus Christ of Latter-day Saints, 1985], 19.

Mighty Change II

1. Hebrews 12: 6.
2. Hebrews 12: 11–13.
3. Matthew 14: 30.
4. 2 Nephi 32: 3.
5. Alma 32: 28.
6. "God Be With You Till We Meet Again," *Hymns of The Church of Jesus Christ of Latter-day Saints* [Salt Lake City: The Church of Jesus Christ of Latter-day Saints, 1985], 152.
7. Alma 7: 11.
8. Neal A. Maxwell, "Willing to Submit," *Ensign*, May 1985, 72.
9. Thomas Wolfe, *Of Time and the River* [New York City: Charles Scribner's Sons, 1935], 332
10. Glenn L. Pace, *Spiritual Plateaus* [Salt Lake City: Deseret Book Co., 1991], 63.
11. *Ibid.,* 77–78.
12. 1 Nephi 8: 11–12.
13. 1 Nephi 11: 22–23.

Mighty Change III

1. Carlfred Broderick, *One Flesh, One Heart* [Salt Lake City: Deseret Book Co., 1986], 79-80.
2. 1 Nephi 3: 7.
3. Glenn L. Pace, "Follow the Prophet," *Ensign*, May 1989.
4. Stephen Robinson, *Following Christ* [Salt Lake City: Deseret Book Co., 1995], 52, 54.
5. See D&C 132: 19.

6. I King 19:11&12.
7. 3 Nephi 9:20.
8. D&C 132:19.
9. D&C 132:19–21.

Mighty Change IV

1. Gordon B. Hinckley, "Stand Strong Against the Wiles of the World," *Ensign*, November 1995, 101.
2. John Kirkland, Fay Deane, Michael Brennan, About CrySOS, a Clinic for People with Crying Babies, *Family Relations* Vol. 32, No. 4 (Oct. 1983), 538.
3. Ludwig Bemelmans, *Madeline* [New York: Simon & Schuster, 1939]
4. Mosiah 24:14.
5. Mark 6:2.
6. Psalm 36:7.

Epilogue

1. Joseph Walker, Woman who had lived lesbian lifestyle brings hope to Mormons with same-sex attraction. *Deseret News* [Salt Lake City, UT] 8 December 2012: A1.
2. Mosiah 27:25–26.
3. David Bednar, "Ye Must Be Born Again," *Ensign*, May 2007, 19.
4. See Moroni 10:32.
5. Mosiah 3:19.
6. Mosiah 5:2.
7. D&C 24:8.

8. Mosiah 3: 19.
9. Lawrence Corbridge, "The Way," *Ensign,* November 2008, 36.
10. 2 Ne. 27: 3.
11. Lawrence Corbridge, "The Way," *Ensign,* November 2008, 34. Note: He used the word "madness" in his address. It was changed to "foolishness" when written for translation purposes.
12. Alma 7: 11–12.
13. D&C 29: 32.
14. D&C 29: 35.
15. Jeffrey R. Holland, "Broken Things to Mend," *Ensign,* May 2006, 69–70.
16. Matthew 19: 26.
17. Lawrence Corbridge, "The Way," *Ensign,* November 2008, 36.
18. Mosiah 3: 19.
19. Acts 4: 32.
20. Moses 7: 18.
21. D&C 105: 3–4.
22. D&C 101: 6.
23. D. Todd Christofferson, "Come to Zion," *Ensign,* November 2008, 38–40.
24. Quoted by David O. McKay, "Pioneer Women," *The Relief Society Magazine,* January 1948, 8.
25. Jeffrey R. Holland, "Prophets in the Land Again," *Ensign,* November 2006, 106–107.
26. *Ibid.,* 107.

20599636R00122

Printed in Great Britain
by Amazon